SINCE LIFE ISN'T A GAME, THESE ARE GOD'S RULES

Finding Joy & Fulfillment in God's Ten Commandments

Kathy Collard Miller

STARBURST PUBLISHERS

P. O. Box 4123, Lancaster, Pennsylvania 17604

To schedule author appearances, write: Author Appearances, Starburst Promotions, P.O. Box 4123, Lancaster, Pennsylvania 17604 or call (717) 293-0939. Website: www.starburstpublishers.com.

CREDITS:
Cover design by Richmond & Williams
Text design and composition by John Reinhardt Book Design

All scripture was taken from the New International Version unless otherwise indicated.

SINCE LIFE ISN'T A GAME, THESE ARE GOD'S RULES
Copyright © 1999 by Kathy Collard Miller
All rights reserved

First Printing, August, 1999

ISBN 1-892016-15-X
Library of Congress Catalog Number: 99-63788
Printed in the United States of America

To
Don and Audrey Miller,
my parents "in-love,"
who graciously allowed me
to steal away their only child.

Thank you for being an example to me
of people who value the Scriptures.

Contents

Preface

In my research for this book I was happy to discover more material about the Ten Commandments recently published than I had expected. Stuart Briscoe's *Playing by the Rules* and R. Kent Hughes' *Disciplines of Grace* were particularly meaningful to me. David A. Seamands' book, *Blueprint for Living*, offered significant food for thought as well.

I also wanted to know what my friends and fellow writers and speakers thought of the Ten Commandments. Was I the only one who thought of them as relevant for today's world? I shouldn't have wondered. When I sent out emails to over six hundred of my correspondents, the response was impressive. Email after email confirmed with declarations and real-life stories the importance of God's ten rules in their own lives.

In order to illustrate particular points in the book, I referred to and quoted from my correspondents' stories. I also shared from the lives of women and men I have met during my speaking engagements. My hope is that the experiences of many will be more instructive than the experiences of one.

I used only the first names of my correspondents, and at times I went so far as to change names to protect the privacy of those who have been open with me about personal matters. I trust you'll find their honesty refreshing and pertinent, for we all lead imperfect lives in an imperfect world.

Acknowledgments

The creative genius of my publisher, David Robie, was instrumental in the wise direction of this concept. My incredible editor, Chad Allen, guided me in crafting the manuscript to be richer and deeper. I'm very grateful to the Starburst staff for all their support. My thanks to Scott Pinzon too!

To those who responded to my cry—"Tell me what the Ten Commandments have meant in your life!?"—I owe my gratitude and affection. Your suggestions and stories have greatly influenced my thinking and the important insights this book offers. Thanks to Karen Dye, Kathryn Presley, Robin Gunn, Christian Ricker, Marie Asner, Todd Anderson, Helen Knueven, Gene Johosky, Suzy Ryan, David and Renee Sanford, Dianne Janak, Alicia Hayden, Mildred Barger, Eva Marie Everson, Anita Anderson, Robin Chaddock, Jeanne Zornes, Irene Carloni, Kurt C. Ward, Diana James, Jean Lewis, Glynis Myers, Carolyn Scheidies, Naomi Rhode, Joan Clayton, DiAnn Mills, Sharie Derrickson, Russell Cox, Bonnie Person, Myrtie Kagey, Stacey Padrick, Elaine Anderson, Jeanie Wise, and Irene Hinkle Faubion.

As always, my love and devotion to my husband, Larry, who is behind every word as he encourages and supports me. Our partnership makes every book his too. Thanks to Darcy and Mark for inquiring about my progress.

And to my readers, thanks for your continuing support. I had you in mind as I wrote this. May you love God more and care more about your fellow man because of the time you spend reading this book.

No *man* is so *happy*
as the real Christian.

BLAISE PASCAL

Introduction

The Ten Commandments are experiencing a new birth of interest in our society. Terry Mattingly, a professor at Milligan College in Tennessee, wrote in his weekly column for the Scripps Howard News Service, "The Ten Commandments are so hot, right now, that it's amazing some Beltway politico hasn't tried to hit Moses with a grand jury subpoena or a blast of rumors about his private life during all those mysterious years out in the desert."

A Gallup poll of youth taken in 1980 found that as many as eight in ten adults and teenagers believe the Ten Commandments are still valid rules for living today.[1]

In the *Los Angeles Times'* "Letters to the Editor" section, Dave Fischer of Irvine, California, wrote, "Is there a relationship between the failure of the House to pass more gun laws and the overwhelming support to have our public schools display the Ten Commandments? Perhaps I'm being naïve but it seems to me that if the American people were willing to guide their lives by these ten simple rules of behavior, we would not need many of the laws we now have."

In June, 1999, the House of Representatives passed a law reinstituting the right of schools to post the Ten Commandments in classrooms.

Interest in morality has intensified with recent news events like the House of Representatives' impeachment of President William Jefferson Clinton and the shooting at Columbine High School in Colorado, not to mention the recent ethnic cleansing in Kosovo.

There are more and more books being published about issues like integrity: the essence of God's ten rules. Stephen Carter, the William Nelson Cromwell Professor of Law at Yale University, is writing three books in a series of what he calls "pre-political virtues," of which the first is his book *Integrity*. He said in an interview,

> We live in a time when people are giving attention, finally, to the spiritual dimensions of public life. Our democratic institutions are at risk precisely because politics has become so relentlessly materialistic, across the political spectrum.
>
> Chuck Colson wrote a piece in the *Wall Street Journal* recently where he mentioned that a warden said to him, "Ten years ago I could talk to these kids about right and wrong. Now they don't know what I'm talking about."
>
> While I'm not a sixties basher, one of the bad things we did in the sixties was to say that all the problems in American society can be traced to repressive traditions. Some people took that as a license to overturn all values in society. So nowadays you have a culture in which, if you simply talk about right and wrong, many people will say that you're being oppressive.[2]

Dr. Laura Schlessinger put a fresh torch to the embers of interest in the Ten Commandments with her book, *The Ten Commandments: The Significance of God's Law in Everyday Life,* which she coauthored with Rabbi Stewart Vogel.

No matter what your views of the Ten Commandments are, it looks as if these "rules" are here to stay for awhile. I, for one, am glad.

Our Source for Joy and Fulfillment

A church ad in a newspaper shows a picture of two hands holding stone tablets on which the Ten Commandments are inscribed. A headline above the tablets reads, "For fast relief take two tablets." Like the tablets we take for overcoming a physical headache, the Ten Commandments are God's prescription for overcoming the spiritual headaches of destructive living.

God clearly, concisely, and convincingly told us how to have integrity, honesty, and, above all, love, in ten statements given to Moses on Mount Sinai. In a little over three hundred words, He who made humankind, knows us intimately, and wants us to be happy set forth ten principles that if practiced bring peace, harmony, and contentment to His creation.

Jesus summed up the Ten Commandments when he said, "As the Father has loved me, so have I loved you. Now remain in my love. If you obey my commands, you will remain in my love, just as I have obeyed my Father's commands and remain in his love. I have told you this so that my joy may be in you and that your joy may be complete" (John 15:9–11). Note how Jesus speaks of love and joy as a direct result of following His commands.

Obedience often seems restrictive, doesn't it? But in this book you'll find obedience gives us the freedom to live the way God intended and to bask in a loving relationship with a Heavenly Father who loves and understands us.

Here are seven benefits we receive from God's ten rules for living.

1. The Ten Commandments let us know God loves us.

It may seem like a funny way for God to express His love, but when God revealed His initial ten ingredients of the Law, He was communicating how much He loved His chosen people—and us.

Before giving the Ten Commandments God brought great catastrophes on the Israelites' captors, the Egyptians. Recall events like all the water turning to blood and the swarms of insects eating everything in sight. As those pestilences overwhelmed the Egyptians, the people of God went unharmed: The blood and insects didn't appear in their territory.

As the Israelites stood trembling in fear at the edge of the formidable Red Sea, watching the Egyptian army come closer and closer, God parted the waters and His people crossed on dry land. The water closed up behind them and their enemies drowned.

As the Israelites began their journey in the wilderness toward God's Promised Land, He miraculously provided manna from the desert floor and water springing out of a rock.

But why? What was it all for?

Shortly before giving His beloved people the Ten Commandments, God told the Israelites, "You yourselves have seen what I did to Egypt, and how I carried you on eagles' wings and brought you to myself. Now if you obey me fully and keep my covenant, then out of all nations you will be my treasured possession. Although the whole earth is mine, you will be for me a kingdom of priests and a holy nation" (Exodus 19:4–6).

Presumably, all God had done for the Israelites—turning the river into blood, sending the swarm of insects, parting the Red Sea, the manna, the water—all of it was leading to the moment when God would give his people the Ten Commandments. As if a great drum roll had been sounded in the heavens, God handed to Moses His rules for the Israelites' joy and fulfillment.

Charles R. Swindoll writes, "In the ancient days of Moses, God was so concerned that His people know His truth that He, with His finger as it were, wrote His laws into stone. Moses brought the stone tablets down from a mountain in his arms. God wanted His people to know His truth."[3]

According to Swindoll, it was *concern* that motivated God to give us His rules, and what is concern if not a very active form of love?

William Law (1686–1761), an English clergyman, wrote: "God has but one intention toward all creation. His purpose is to pour the goodness of his divine perfection upon everything that is capable of receiving it."[4]

The Ten Commandments are one of the best examples of the "goodness" of God's "divine perfection." They are, in fact, a demonstration of God's love.

2. The Ten Commandments show us how to express our love for God.

The Israelites didn't view God's commands as good for them. They didn't view their God as a loving God who wanted their best. As a result, they "stood at a distance" and weren't able to fulfill their God-given purpose to love God in return (Exodus 20:18–19). But that wasn't God's intention at all. God's rules are meant for our good, to reveal His goodness. Richard C. Halverson, former chaplain to the Senate, writes: "These commandments are not arbitrary statutes handed down by a power-hungry despot. They are the clearest, most fundamental design for social order...the most precise description of reality as God created it to be. When conformed to, they represent life at its best, individually and socially."[5]

Many years after the giving of the Law at Sinai, Jesus spelled out God's intention by saying, "If you love me, you will obey what I command" (John 14:15). Those were the words of Jesus shortly before He left this earth to be with His Father. Earlier, when Jesus was asked, "Which is the greatest commandment in the Law?" He replied, "'Love the Lord your God with all your heart and with all your soul and with all your mind.' This is the first and greatest commandment. And the second is like it: 'Love your neighbor as yourself'" (Matthew 22:36–39).

I've had the same kind of fear and skepticism as the Israelites. As a little girl, I believed God was looking down at me, His arms crossed over His chest as He tapped his foot, saying impatiently, "Kathy, when are you going to become perfect so that I can really love you?" I believed God wanted me to perform perfectly so that He could accept me. When I tried to act perfectly and continually failed, I felt hopeless, wondering how I'd ever earn my way into heaven. And when bad things happened to me, I concluded that God had given up on me. Over time that hopelessness turned into an anger that I would eventually inflict upon my family, even to the point of physically abusing my two-year-old daughter. I felt frustrated because I kept asking for God's instantaneous deliverance. When He didn't answer my prayer the way I thought He should, I believed He had stopped loving me.

I couldn't see God's love for me and neither could the Israelites. When God delayed delivering them while they were in Egypt, they blamed Moses and Aaron. When they had to find their own straw to make the bricks, they didn't think God loved them. They looked at how God was working and didn't approve of His method. To them, His delay was His denial. They withdrew in fear when God tried to reveal His love. All they could think about were their own needs rather than going beyond their selfishness to loving God.

Moses, on the other hand, met personally with God and got to know intimately His desire to bless His people. Moses knew God's goodness and could love God by obeying Him. Famous Catholic mystic Bernard of Clairvaux wrote, "Personal familiarity with God's goodness is the best incentive to pure love of him."[6]

I was like the Israelites, fearful and skeptical of God, when I was in that pit of anger. I'm glad that God corrected my wrong ideas about Him, and I'm glad he showed me how He wanted to deliver me from my anger. He didn't want to deliver me instantaneously. He wanted to take me through a process of growth so that I could learn biblical principles that could then be passed along to others. My perspective of God changed to something more like that of Moses. I began to understand that God hadn't given up on me, that He still loved me. Then I could love Him back in great gratitude for His incredible work in my life.

Moses must have been surprised at the people's reaction to God. He had met with the Almighty God of the Universe and found God only wanted the best for His people. Moses wanted their fear to turn to reverence and tried to help them see that the purpose of the Commandments was to give them a challenge: to test their loyalty to God. If they would rise to the occasion, they would be filled with love and appreciation for God as they depended on Him and received His strength to obey.

Gwen Shamblin, author of *The Weigh Down Diet*, writes, "These are easy commandments from this wonderful God. We should praise Him that salvation (being able to enter His presence) is not performance-based. We just need to love Him, and we can do this! If you truly love, it is not a performance or a drama—it is simply natural. If your love is golf, how hard is it to go play a game? Would you call a game of golf work? Of course not."[7]

As you and I understand our God's love for us, we will become like Moses: trusting that God really loves us and then seeing His acts in light of that love. Even if God delays His answers or doesn't answer our prayers the way we'd like, we will still want to obey and love Him because we know that He wants only our best. Obeying the Ten Commandments will be our way of responding in love out of great gratitude.

3. The Ten Commandments reveal our need for a Savior.

The Ten Commandments were intended to draw us closer to God; they were never meant as criteria for salvation. We shouldn't be tempted to think that keeping them will earn our way into heaven. Pastor James Olson of Faith Evangelical Free Church in Fort Collins, Colorado, says the Ten Commandments are like a mirror that reveals who we truly are and thereby helps us to see our need for God: "Keeping the Ten Commandments is not the way we become Christians, but it is a way to identify us as Christians," Olson says.

When you and I look at the Ten Commandments and realize how difficult it is to keep all of them perfectly, God nods his approval and says, "Yes! That's exactly what I want you to feel. When you realize you can't do it in your own power, you will be pressed to depend upon Me."

Author and theologian John Stott says, "Not until the law has bruised and smitten us will we admit our need for the gospel to bind up our wounds. Not until the law has arrested and imprisoned us will we pine for Christ to set us free. Not until the law has condemned and killed us will we call upon Christ for justification and life. Not until the law has driven us to despair of ourselves will we ever believe in Jesus."[8]

God meant His laws to be simple and uncomplicated for the ancient Hebrews, revealing the way to fulfillment. But in time, the religious leaders, those who were supposed to help the Hebrews keep the law, made the law so complicated that it brought discouragement instead of hope.

For instance, author Joy Davidman, who was C. S. Lewis's wife, explains how the Israelites misinterpreted the Ten Commandments:

> To keep the Sabbath holy, ultimately, meant obeying 1,521 different blue laws—for example, you had to remove your false teeth. To keep the name of God holy, you had to give up using it altogether; eventually its very syllables were forgotten. The frightened men of Christ's day, groaning under the intolerable social security of the Roman peace, turned to their law and found only a tangle of gobbledygook. Like us, they could obey it blindly or reject it blindly; but they could not possibly make sense of it.[9]

Although the Jewish Pharisees made the Law complicated, God offers to help us to obey Him in simple love. Charles R. Swindoll says it this way. "Our propensity is to sin. So why did God give the law if He knew we couldn't keep it? First, the law illustrates God's character. God is holy, good, pure, righteous. We, however, are not, which the law reveals quite clearly. We must obtain holiness, goodness, purity, and righteousness from an outside source . . . from God Himself. So a second purpose of the law is to make us aware of our own sinfulness and drive us to Christ, from whom we receive cleansing from sin and right standing before God."[10]

As we recognize our need for Jesus and make Him Lord of our minds and hearts, all we need to do is surrender and say, "God, do it within me," and then He provides the inner workings to respond.

This principle of surrender was modeled for me some time ago by a scene I saw in the park. A young couple and their three-year-old son were training their German Shepherd puppy. The husband and wife stood about fifty feet apart, and the husband called the dog, "Lucky, come!" while bringing his arm toward his chest, which was the signal they were using to reinforce their verbal commands. Lucky bounded over to the man and was rewarded with petting. Then the wife did the same thing, and Lucky ran to her.

The little boy joined them. He called to the dog and awkwardly tried to imitate the motion his parents had made. Lucky stared at the boy, took a few steps, and sat down. The boy called again but Lucky hesitated.

Then, without the boy realizing it, the father silently moved behind him and motioned with his arm as the boy called, "Lucky, come!" Lucky immediately ran toward the child on his way to the father. The little boy jumped up and down with delight, hugging the dog, believing Lucky had obeyed his commands.

It's the same as we live in God's power. All we have to do is "make the right motions" by being willing to follow Him. God will do the rest. The result will be obedience, not because of our own power, but because God is within us, strengthening us to keep His commandments.

We may feel like we are making things happen, but the Spirit is really the one who does all the heavy lifting. As we recognize our need for Jesus and ask for the Holy Spirit's power, it is as if God is silently waving His hand on our behalf, and we are able to obey what formerly had been impossible.

4. The Ten Commandments mark us off as "peculiar people."

God wanted the Israelites' obedience to the Ten Commandments to be the "mark" upon their lives that would cause unbelievers to point to them and say, "Oh, yeah, those people are the ones for whom God has done so much. They sure are a joyful group, aren't they? I want to get to know them and their God." In the same way, we want those who don't know the Lord to call us "peculiar," meaning "distinct, different, and set apart."

Christian philosopher Francis Schaeffer wrote:

Through the centuries, people have displayed many different symbols to show that they are Christians. They have worn marks in the lapels of their coats, hung chains about their necks, even had special haircuts.

Of course, there is nothing wrong with any of this, if one feels it is his calling. But there is a much better sign— a mark that has not been thought up just as a matter of expediency for use on some special occasion or in some specific era. It is a universal mark that is to last through all the ages of the church till Jesus comes back.

What is this mark? At the close of his ministry, Jesus looks forward to his death on the cross, the open tomb, and the ascension. Knowing that he is about to leave, Jesus makes clear what will be the distinguishing mark of the Christian:

My children, I will be with you only a little longer. You will look for me, and just as I told the Jews, so I tell you now: Where I am going, you cannot come.

> A new command I give you: Love one another. As
> I have loved you, so you must love one another. By
> this all men will know that you are my disciples, if
> you love one another. (John 13:33–35) [11]

When God gave His chosen people the Ten Commandments, He was giving them instructions for loving Himself—according to His definition of love—and to love other people. Those rules were unique in all of the cultures the Israelites had known or would know. God tells them to be different. Instead of worshiping many gods like other people, He told them to worship only Himself. Instead of being selfish like the people around them, the Israelites should be loving. This was the mark that would distinguish them. It is also the mark that will distinguish us.

Ronald B. Allen, professor of Hebrew Scripture at West Baptist Seminary in Portland, Oregon, and author of *Lord of Song: Discovering the Messiah in the Psalms*, writes:

> Amazingly, when we think about it, God gave His people His Law directly after He had delivered them from slavery in Egypt. Just as He was in the process of making the company of slaves into a free people, and that people into His own people, God gave the Law as His gift of independence. They were independent of oppressors and now free to live as His people, His particular community. The Law would be their guide.
>
> The law was His gift to help them to order their lives as His peculiar people, to direct their affairs as His distinct community. [12]

5. The Ten Commandments keep us safe.

We tend to think freedom is not having any rules. We think freedom is doing whatever we want. But whenever I begin thinking that way, I remember an incident I heard about many years ago. During some construction at an elementary school, the fence around the schoolyard had to be removed. The teachers wondered how the children would react as they played on the swings that bordered where the fence had separated them from a street. Some of the teachers wondered whether the removal of the fence would actually give the children a sense of freedom. They argued that the fence gave a restrictive atmosphere to the playground. Everyone was eager to watch the children's reaction.

When the children were dismissed for their first recess, the teachers were amazed to see them huddled near the school buildings. They wouldn't even go close to the swings. They were afraid because the fence no longer protected them from the street beyond.

You and I may long for complete freedom from God's rules, but God's rules actually give us security. They keep us safe. They give us the freedom to know exactly what God expects, and then, as He provides the strength to obey His rules, we experience success. Those are God's valuable gifts: the resources we need to obey and the rewards for having obeyed.

My friend Mel talks about the rules his mother had when he was four years old. He wanted to run away from home, but his mom's rules said he couldn't cross the street. So he went to the front yard and sat under a tree with the lunch his mom had packed. He quips, "My lower lip was so big from pouting that I wasn't sure if a bird flying by was trying to land on it, but I was glad when supper time came. And since my ability to remember why I was on the front lawn was no longer important, I was happy to hear Mom call, 'It's time to eat.'"

That night as Mel's mom tucked him into bed and gave him a big hug, he was thankful for the rule: "Don't cross the street."

Mel explains, "Just like Mom, God has rules to protect us. And sometimes in the race of life, we break some of the rules, but I will always be Mom's son . . . and God's son."

There is security in God's rules. If Mel's mom hadn't kept

him on the front lawn with her rule, he may have run away and found himself in serious danger.

As our loving Father watches over us, He directs our way to joy and fulfillment through His rules. Without His guidelines we would feel insecure. Imagine for a moment that the Bible hadn't been written, yet you had a sense of God and wanted to please him. Would you not often pray, "I don't know the right way! What do you want me to do, Lord? What will please you?"

The next time you begin to be disgruntled about the seeming restrictions of the Ten Commandments, remember those children huddled by the fence. Without God's instructions you would feel insecure, afraid to do the wrong thing. And without God's rules, other people could feel free to do to you whatever they wish. We are truly blessed!

6. The Ten Commandments equip us to represent God to other people.

God chose His people Israel for a very special purpose: to represent Him to the world. Even though they were imperfect, God knew He could bring glory to Himself through them. As His children, you and I are called to do the same thing. Paul wrote, "We are therefore Christ's ambassadors, as though God were making his appeal through us. We implore you on Christ's behalf: Be reconciled to God" (2 Corinthians 5:20). Our job description is to represent the holy God we serve, and God's ten rules for living are the best way we can live in a way that says, "I'm God's child."

Whenever his kingdom had been victorious, Alexander the Great had a custom of marching his army in front of himself. In this way he would would bestow praise and honor on his valiant troops, but the custom didn't end there. After the victory march all of the men who had turned tail in battle would be brought before the king. His sentence for each was always the same: death.

Imagine soldier after soldier walking with trembling fear

up to the king, pleading to him for mercy, and imagine every time the immediately obeyed sentence of that powerful man: "Death!"

On one such occasion the last deserter to be brought before the king was a young boy. Intrigued, Alexander inquired after him. As it turns out, this boy had actually been very brave; he had fought with all the other soldiers until, right at the end of a battle when things were getting fiercer than ever, the boy ran away.

Hearing the story, the king leaned back in his chair, looked at the young fellow, and asked, "Boy, what is your name?"

The frightened boy whispered, "My name is Alexander, sir."

The king rose to the edge of his seat and repeated the question with force, "Boy, I asked you, what is your name?"

The boy answered, "Alexander, sir. My parents named me after you."

The king stood up, "Boy! What is your name?"

And the boy with tears in his eyes looked at the king and said, "My name is Alexander."

Alexander the Great resumed his throne saying, "Boy, either change your name, or change your ways."

If we dare call ourselves Christians, we have an obligation to be ambassadors of our God. Following the Ten Commandments will ensure that we live up to that obligation.

7. The Ten Commandments are God's recipe for true success.

The "success" God promises us through obeying His commandments does not conform to the world's definition. God's success is on a higher level.

My friend Stephanie is a missionary to Taiwan, and while on a short-term missionary trip to Malaysia, she was asked by the local leadership of a church to share whatever God might place on her heart at the next meeting, where many non-Christians would attend. She really didn't want to because she had recently experienced the loss of her beloved brother and always felt on the edge of tears. She was afraid she might break down at any time—especially when speaking in front of a group. Even though they asked her to pray about it, she had already decided God would say "no."

But when she hesitantly turned her attention to Him with a token request for guidance, she was shocked to hear Him say, "Do it." She started to pray in earnest. After two hours of seeking the Lord's direction, she heard Him say, "Tell them about Rick's life."

She couldn't believe it. Rick? Rick, her brother, who had recently died of cancer? Stephanie was still grieving deeply. "Oh, Lord," she cried out. "I can't! I just can't! I can't talk about Rick without crying. What good will it do for me to stand up in front of all those non-Christians and not be able to talk because I'm sobbing!"

But God's quiet message did not change. After another hour of prayer, Stephanie knew she was facing a choice. She could either obey or refuse. It was as simple as that. When she surrendered, God clearly gave her the message she should tell. She should contrast her brother with her father.

That night, Stephanie stood in front of a group of Christians and non-Christians and first told them about her father who was a talented CIA agent. She explained, "My father did many exciting things as an agent and then became a successful businessman. Yet as he died, he talked only of how his life was full of regrets. He had put his priorities in all the wrong things and he recognized it.

"But the other man I want to tell you about is my brother, Rick," she went on to say. "He went through a horrible struggle with drugs and alcohol until he turned his life over to Christ. But when Rick began to walk with Jesus, he came alive. He sang in church, reached out to others, and helped them in practical ways.

"Then two years ago, Rick got cancer." Stephanie's voice

began to lose volume. "Yet, he was grateful even for that because it helped him understand how much God loved him."

Stephanie didn't know if she could continue talking. The memories of Rick flooded through her mind and she felt as if her heart was breaking. Then she looked over at the high school students who had accompanied her on the missions trip. They were holding hands and praying. A new sense of peace filled her heart and she knew she could go on.

"Rick suffered a great deal as he died slowly, yet he wanted to be awake so that he could be available to people. Even as he was in great pain, he kept praising God. And then, finally, he mouthed the words to his favorite praise chorus, smiled, and died. Everyone at the funeral talked about how much Rick had done for other people. Not a single person talked about Rick's job or how much money he made. They talked about eternal values and how he had showed them the love and peace of Jesus."

As Stephanie looked out over the Malaysian people, she concluded with a statement and question we should all take to heart: "How we die will depend on what choices we make while we live. Do you want to experience a kind of life and death like my father's, or a life and death like my brother's?"

Search Yourself

Are the Ten Commandments restrictive-sounding to you or do they represent freedom? What should they represent?

⁓✲⁓

Can you name the Ten Commandments from memory?

⁓✲⁓

Which commandments are easy for you to follow and which ones are difficult? Why?

⁓✲⁓

Which of the seven above-mentioned benefits best help you to see why God gave us the Ten Commandments?

⁓✲⁓

What benefits would you like to experience in your life as a result of obeying the Ten Commandments?

⁓✲⁓

What do you hope to gain from reading this book?

We should give God
the same place in our hearts
that he holds
in the universe.

CICERO

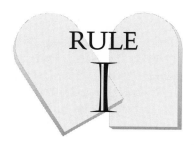

RULE
I

Worship God and God Alone

I AM THE LORD YOUR GOD . . .
YOU SHALL HAVE NO OTHER GODS BEFORE ME.

Exodus 20:2, 3

The sun peeked softly from behind the drapes and I stretched, throwing the bedcovers off. "Oh, god of the day, cause this day to go smoothly," I prayed.

Moments later, I shuffled into the kitchen and poured a cup of coffee. I mentally rehearsed my speech for the morning meeting. "Oh, god of intellect, help me to remember it."

As I braved the traffic on the way to the office, I gripped the steering wheel and complained all the way. Then I fearfully remembered the wrath of the god of traffic from the traffic accident I'd had last month. Penitently, I cried out, "Oh, god of traffic, I'm sorry. If I've displeased you, I apologize. You are always good."

Walking into the office, my secretary looked up from her desk, startled. "Oh, I've got bad news. Your contact for your sales meeting this afternoon canceled. He's going to buy from Phillips Industries instead."

I gave her a withering look. I knew it wasn't her fault, but I sure couldn't blame the god of business, otherwise he'd get back at me another way. I must have displeased him somehow. Now what did I do? Oh, that must be it: I didn't ask him to be in charge of the day. Now I knew he was more powerful than the god of the day, so I'd have to pray to him first when I woke up.

I slammed my briefcase down on the desk and vowed to try to remember the pecking order of the gods so that nothing else bad would happen that day.

Can you imagine living like that? Although it seems impossible to our modern minds, if God had not revealed Himself and the old beliefs had continued to this day, that is exactly how you and I may have wound up today:

- never knowing who was in charge
- never knowing what god we had made angry
- never knowing how to please a god who didn't reveal himself or herself
- always trying to interpret the bad things that happened

Doesn't sound pleasant, does it?

Thank Heaven, There's Only One God

You and I don't have to live that way, and God doesn't want us to. He prevented us from doing so by revealing Himself and saying, "I'm the only God there is."

That is the essence of the First Commandment. When a person believes in many gods, he can be sent in many directions all at once. But when a person believes in the Christian God who isn't subject to mood swings and has only one will, that person doesn't have to wonder whether what will please him at one point will continue to please Him. What a relief!

Such relief isn't as strong as it would be if we could truly imagine what worshiping many gods would be like. John Timmerman, author of *Do We Still Need the Ten Commandments?*, explains,

> The Israelites lived as God's chosen people in a culture marked by polytheism [a belief in many gods] and idolatry [a belief in a material object representing a deity and worshiped as such]. The people all around them served many gods: they had a god for crops, a god for household affairs, for good weather, for curses or blessings, for war, for peace. They were a busy people, keeping all those gods satisfied. And it was also very confusing. Who finally rules? Who has final say? Who bears authority? The people must have gone wild worshiping all their gods. [1]

Their lives must have been characterized by worry, nervousness, and strife. Joy Davidman writes: "The old gods fought among themselves, loved and hated without reason, demanded unspeakable bribes and meaningless flatteries. While they were worshiped, a moral law was impossible, for what pleased one deity would offend another." [2]

One of the most easily offended and most evil gods was Molech, who was particularly known for requiring horrible offerings. Of course, Molech didn't truly communicate that because he wasn't real. But that is what came from man's imagination. As a result, the idol makers built a hollow metal statue of Molech and built a fire inside. When the metal was hot enough, a child was placed on the searing outstretched arms of the statue. Life was cheap in the shadow of such a god. What must those people have thought when even after the sacrifice of a child, bad things *still* happened?

John H. Timmerman explains, "These gods were invented by humans to meet human needs, in humanity's image. Certain sacrifices, these people believed, would persuade the gods to respond to those human needs. Humans tried to manipulate the divine powers for their own advantage. Never was there a personal relationship between god and humans; always it was an issue of power." [3]

No Substitutes

We can't really look down our noses at the people of those times. In many ways, we do the same things, sometimes even emotionally sacrificing humans to get our needs met.

Shortly after God gave the Israelites the Ten Commandments, Moses returned to the mountain to commune with God. When he was gone longer than the impatient Israelites wanted to wait, they said to Aaron, "Come, make us gods who will go before us. As for this fellow Moses who brought us up out of Egypt, we don't know what has happened to him" (Exodus 32:1).

They wanted a god they could touch. A god who did their bidding. They did not want the Jehovah God who kept them waiting. Maybe God had even killed Moses. Were they going to have to wait forever? And since they couldn't control what God did, they encouraged Aaron to provide a tangible deity whom they could control with their own set of beliefs.

Note, however, that the Israelites did recognize they needed something outside of themselves to meet their needs. Alan

Redpath, author of *Law and Liberty: The Ten Commandments for Today*, writes, "Every man must have a god. There is really no such person as an atheist, for such a man worships himself and the material world. There is no human being without a shrine in his heart where there is a god whom he worships. The very composition of human life demands a center of worship as a necessity of existence."[4]

We set up our own center of worship whenever we try to get our needs met in other ways, in our own timing and in our own method. But God wants to meet them in His way, His timing, and His method.

God gave us our needs so that we would long for Him. Dr. Larry Crabb identifies these needs in his book, *Effective Biblical Counseling*: "The most basic need is a sense of personal worth, an acceptance of oneself as a whole, real person. The two required inputs are *significance* (purpose, importance, adequacy for a job, meaningfulness, impact) and *security* (love—unconditional and consistently expressed; permanent acceptance)."[5]

God intended us to find significance in calling ourselves children of God and appreciating the inheritance He gave us through Christ. He offers us the unconditional love that we were designed to crave, but we often seek substitutes for our craving.

Addictions

A "god" in the form of addictions can erupt within our priorities. One form might be the things we are passionate about, another could be preoccupations, and a third, pleasures of the body. Each becomes a focus that displaces God's rightful place as our only God.

Marie* identified for me how she had a passion for music. Her recital became her passionate goal but an unsatisfying god.

---

*As mentioned in the preface, I will use first names only when referring to my corrrespondents.

As a child growing up under the loving tutelage of a mother who was a musician, Marie eagerly looked forward to her recital. Over many years as a child she took intermediate steps to prepare for the ultimate recital at age eighteen.

She says, "At age eighteen, when the recital came and went, I felt empty. Was that all there was? This 'god' didn't satisfy or give comfort, instead it demanded more and more. I learned that having an all-consuming passion or goal is just that—all-consuming. There is nothing left for life and for praising the One who gave me the talent. I had, indeed, put 'another god' before Him. But in time I surrendered to the One who counted. Now I know talent is to be used for His glory in living a God-filled life."

Another source of a "god" is preoccupation. Many people live for activities like sports. Whether it's watching it vicariously on TV, attending games in person, or participating themselves, sports can be a preoccupation that makes people feel alive.

If ever there was a man who was dedicated to a sport, it was Tom Landry, a very successful coach of the Dallas Cowboys football team. He was the Cowboys' only head coach in the team's first twenty-nine years of existence. But then in February, 1989, Tom found out through a television announcement that the Cowboys had been sold and a new coach would replace him. His forty-year career in professional football came to a sudden end.

Yet, somehow, Tom prevented football from becoming a "god" by making his true God, the Lord Jesus Christ, his number one priority. He says, "After I made a personal commitment to Christ in 1959, the biggest effect my faith had on me was in the area of priorities. I've spent the rest of my life since then working at God's priorities—putting him first, putting my wife and family second and making my career third. That became my goal, even though I didn't always do as well as I wanted to do in keeping that perspective."

That perspective was tested as Landry was fired. How would

he do without football in his life? Would he miss it? He explained, "I do miss the interaction with players and coaches, and the challenge of creating and executing a game plan. But I see very clearly how God was preparing me for this new stage of life." [6] Although it can be a struggle, even the sports "god" can be put in its rightful place.

Pleasures of the body are another form of a "god." Gene knows the pain of making alcohol into a god. He says,

I was so deeply engrossed in an alcohol habit, I'm now convinced I made alcohol a god which I put before anything or anybody else. By giving priority in my life to drinking, I certainly placed my habit above everything else of importance—whether my wife, family, friends, or even work. Everything I did had to be alcohol-centered. If it weren't, I would simply choose not to become involved.

Only by putting God and my obedience to Him above everything else was I able to unsnarl myself from the trap in which I had become enslaved. Only by not allowing anything to come before God could I muster the internal fortitude that was necessary to defeat my habit of alcoholism.

Regardless of the addictions that could become more important than our true God, God is stronger than any of those powerful "gods."

Perfectionism and People Pleasing

Some gods are more subtle than addictions. Two examples are perfectionism and people pleasing.

Suzy, a young mom living in Southern California, made her "god" becoming the perfect mom. She couldn't leave her children with anyone for fear they wouldn't be treated the way she could take care of them. They were more important to her than obeying God—until He challenged her with an opportunity to become involved in the leadership of Bible Study Fellowship, an international organization offering Bible study programs. But becoming a part of BSF's leadership would require Suzy to leave her children in the child care program more than she ever had before.

Suzy explains, "I prayed about the commitment, and knew the Lord had called me into this ministry. Although I had to find a babysitter for my youngest child (six months old), my other two children (three and two) loved the program. Looking back, I see God's fingerprints directing this decision in my life. I only left my children out of obedience to God, but He used BSF to heal me from making my children like gods in my life."

People pleasing is another subtle "god" we can worship. This god's insidious control over our lives often makes it difficult for us to identify its influence. That was certainly the case for Dianne. Because of the dysfunction of her family in her growing-up years, she tried to please people in order to feel loved and important. When she sensed she had indeed made others happy with her, she felt good about herself. That "high" (as she describes it) was the substitute for the legitimate fellowship God wants us to have with other Christians. God faithfully brought healing in Dianne's life, and today she isn't controlled by people pleasing as she was in the past. But is she cured?

She says,

I am constantly having to correct my tendency to start people pleasing again. It's such a natural temptation for me to fall into. I love relationships and people, and I have to constantly put God above this love or eventually I will get wounded and hurt, or I will be the one who disappoints and hurts another.

This is not like abstaining from alcohol or gambling or a spending-spree addiction because God mandates us to love others and be in fellowship with them. Therefore, I can't separate myself completely from people so that I won't be tempted.

Instead, it's a constant struggle to keep my priorities in place. But I'm learning to seek His approval and please Him.

Those of us who sometimes succumb to the god of people pleasing can take encouragement from Dianne's experience. In order to do that, we'll need to remember that even good things like wanting to do things perfectly and pleasing others can become "gods."

Problems and Pride

There are other subtle "gods" that jump up and down in front of us, clamoring for our attention and devotion. Two of them are problems and pride.

It may seem strange to think of problems as being a "god." After all, most of us would say we try to avoid problems. We want to solve them as quickly as possible. Although that's true, Alicia wisely warns us that problems can become a god—when we let them control us.

She says,

Worrying and obsessing over our problems doesn't show any trust in the Lord's ability to handle everything. When I was really struggling with problems at work, a friend in my Christian business group gave me a sheet of paper that read "Good Morning! This is God. I will be handling all your problems today. I will not need your help. So, have a good day!"

That really struck a cord with me. It is our Lord Jesus that watches over us and brings all things together for the good of the Kingdom. I'm reminded to not let my problems become a god. Instead I can let God handle them.

For Alicia, one of the keys to doing that is through her written prayer journal. As she keeps track of how God has worked in her life, she can trust Him for the current problems that seem overwhelming. Her faith and dependence grow through reviewing His faithfulness in the past.

Now she can say, "When I seek Him first for all my worries, thank Him for all He has blessed me with, trust Him infinitely, and lovingly surrender in obedience to Him, I am keeping God first. He is truly my real God then."

How about our reputations? Shouldn't God want our reputation to be good so that we can rightly represent Him? That would make sense—until even our reputation becomes more important than Him. Then it becomes an excuse for pride.

Eva Marie was challenged in this area when she worked on several projects at a Christian organization and wasn't given the credit for it. Her superior passed along her creative ideas and took credit for them himself.

She says, "I was both hurt and angry! I had to get to the place where I realized that who expressed the ideas didn't matter. It didn't matter that someone else claimed them, either. Because, in reality, they were placed in my heart by God for His purposes—not for mine."

But that wasn't the end of the story. After Eva Marie learned to surrender her need to be credited, the top boss came to her and said, "I want you to know that I knew it was you all along."

She was surprised when his comment didn't make her happy. "I realized then that it wasn't truly *me* that deserved the credit. It was God! I don't ever want my reputation or pride to become my god again!"

A Choice Worth Repeating

If God told you to give away your car, how would you feel?

If God told you to surrender the need to control your daughter's life, how would you feel?

If God told you to quit your job and become a missionary, how would you feel?

What one thing would you literally hate to give up? Could

it be that *that* is your god? Christian philosopher Albert Schweitzer said, "If you own something you cannot give away, then you don't own it—it owns you."

Alan Redpath thinks only God should have that place: ". . . our God is the person we think most precious, for whom we would make the greatest sacrifice, and who moves our hearts with the warmest love. He is the person who, if we lost Him, would leave us desolate."[7]

Yet, what right does God have to require that I surrender everything to Him? Why is making Him my only God so important? Does He *need* me to do that?

No, God doesn't need any of us. Martin Bucer, a sixteenth-century German monk who was a supporter and friend of Martin Luther, wrote: "God does not need our service. God is complete in himself. He can do without us. His divinity is independent of our existence. The reason God made us and all other creatures is to make his goodness known."[8]

Plus, God has earned the privilege of asking us to give our all to Him, to let Him be our only God. Paul wrote, "Do you not know that your body is a temple of the Holy Spirit, who is in you, whom you have received from God? You are not your own; you were bought at a price. Therefore honor God with your body" (I Corinthians 6:19–20).

We are truly foolish not to surrender to such a wonderful God. Dr. Laura Schlessinger writes,

At the time of the Ten Commandments (approximately 1300 B.C.E.), the idea of an obligation to *one* God was unique. Instead of allegiances to many gods who had conflicting roles in the world, and whose all-too-human moods and behaviors blurred the absoluteness of right and wrong, monotheism (belief in one God) posited a single, objective morality. The Israelites were told that they need not be confused like children with parents who cannot agree on consistent rules because they're battling each other for power and love. Instead, by acknowledging the One true God, what was required would be clear. [9]

Unlike the worshipers of gods such as Molech and other capricious gods made with human hands, you and I can be secure, knowing that God will meet our true needs because of His goodness and love. But how do we surrender those things that we *think* will meet our needs? Kurt gives us one key when he says, "Keeping God first is nothing more than letting Him tell me where to go, what to say, and how to act. Those three things shape my life and my living according to His will."

Hebrews 12:2 describes Kurt's thought this way: "Let us fix our eyes on Jesus, the author and perfecter of our faith, who for the joy set before him endured the cross, scorning its shame, and sat down at the right hand of the throne of God. Consider him who endured such opposition from sinful men, so that you will not grow weary and lose heart."

The word *fix* refers to a constant, moment-by-moment choice. Although we initially make God our Savior when we ask Jesus to cleanse us from our sin, the daily living out of that commitment is not done all at once. It's not a once-and-forever thing. Over and over again we make that choice of worshiping the Lord as our only God.

Martin Luther said, "I did not learn my theology all at once, but I had to search deeper for it, where my temptations took me. . . . Not understanding, reading, or speculation, but living— nay, dying and being damned—make a theologian."

Martin Luther went through that process; so can we. And God isn't upset that it takes time. Paul writes to the Philippians with that same kind of good news. He wrote, "being confident of this, that he who began a good work in you will carry it on to completion until the day of Christ Jesus" (Philippians 1:6).

Paul recognized God works within us, and God isn't in a hurry. He'll continue the process until we join Him in heaven.

Hold Loosely Those False Gods

Another principle for making God our only God is to hold loosely the things that clamor to gain our allegiance instead of Him. Charles Swindoll reports how Corrie ten Boom gave him the key to doing that. "I'll never forget a conversation I had with the late Corrie ten Boom. She said to me, in her broken English, 'Chuck, I've learned that we must hold everything loosely, because when I grip it tightly, it hurts when the Father pries my fingers loose and takes it from me!' Things of significant value are the unseen things, aren't they? But that is easy to forget." [10]

My sister Karen shared a concept with me that has helped me to hold things loosely and make God my priority. She explained to me,

I see our lives as the Master Menu on a computer. As we scan the icons of the Master Menu, there are icons labeled self, money, spouse, career, parents, and many other unique icons for each person. Nestled within those icons is the icon for "Lord."

When God isn't our *only* God, we see Him as just another source listed on that Master Menu. But if we come to God first instead of moving through and trusting in the other resources in our lives—those other icons—we would save ourselves much grief and heartache. There should be only one icon on the Master Menu and that should be "Lord." When we click onto that, another screen opens and He offers more resources, directed by His wisdom and empowered by His Spirit. He will show us how He wants each situation to be dealt with in relation to the other resources in our lives. If we refuse to accept what God has given us, we lose out on the fullness of God's best for us. If we truly believe He is Lord and sovereign and that He loves us, then we must accept that all of His ways and purposes are perfect.

As soon as we recognize something is becoming too important, we can realize we've placed a new icon on our mind's Master Menu. Then we need to say as Jesus modeled for us, "Not my will, but thine be done." We might envision laying that thing or person on an altar or imagine Jesus standing in front of us with His arms outstretched, waiting for us to hand the item over. That will remove the icon from the Master Menu of our lives and replace it with the "Lord" icon.

Theologian J. I. Packer gives us some practical advice: "Our part is to accept the triune Jehovah as our God; to ask, and depend on him daily, for whatever we need; to pledge our loyal obedience, and keep our promise in his strength; to aim in all we do at pleasing him; and constantly to practice repentance, which starts with confessing and apologizing for our sins and ends with renouncing them and asking to be delivered from them." [11]

Is anything more important than making God your *only* God? You can't go wrong to trust a God who wants only your good.

Search Yourself

What gods, other than the true God, do you recognize as vying for your time and attention on the Master Menu of your life?

※

Why are those "gods" seemingly so important and attractive?

※

What needs do each of them seem to meet? How do you feel when they don't meet your needs?

※

How does God meet your needs better?

※

What does it mean to make God "first?"

※

How do you make God "first" in practical ways?

Let God be God.

MARTIN LUTHER

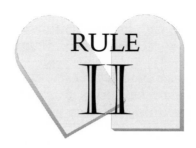

RULE

II

Set Your Priorities in Stone

YOU SHALL NOT MAKE FOR YOURSELF AN IDOL IN THE
FORM OF ANYTHING IN HEAVEN ABOVE OR ON THE
EARTH BENEATH OR IN THE WATERS BELOW. YOU SHALL
NOT BOW DOWN TO THEM OR WORSHIP THEM; FOR I,
THE LORD YOUR GOD, AM A JEALOUS GOD, PUNISHING
THE CHILDREN FOR THE SIN OF THE FATHERS TO THE
THIRD AND FOURTH GENERATION OF THOSE WHO
HATE ME, BUT SHOWING LOVE TO A THOUSAND
[GENERATIONS] OF THOSE WHO LOVE ME
AND KEEP MY COMMANDMENTS.

EXODUS 20:4–6

Driving down a steep California mountain in December,
as snow lined the sides of the highway, I thanked God
that the storm had stopped long enough for the roads to
be clear. As I neared a bend in the two-lane highway, a

man stood on the other side of the road facing me, motioning repeatedly with his hands palms out.

"What is that crazy man doing?" I mumbled. "What does he mean?"

Then his message suddenly became clear. He was trying to tell me to slow down. I eased up on the accelerator and the car slowed. Around the corner was a line of cars crawling by an accident. My obedience to the man's signal had prevented me from slamming into the back end of a Toyota Celica. Needless to say, I was grateful for the man's warning.

The Ten Commandments are like that kind man. They tell us to slow down. They warn us about the wrong ways we might worship God or try to get to know Him.

Originally I didn't recognize the man's good intentions or the important message he wanted to communicate. If I had continued only to think of him as "crazy" and not paid attention to his signal, I would have met with disaster.

In the same way we may doubt God's good intentions when we read the Ten Commandments. We may even think He has a few screws loose.

Maybe that's how the ancient Hebrews felt when God gave them this second rule. It was so unnatural and different from the beliefs all around them. Some of them must have scratched their heads, wondering, "What in the world is going on with God? Is He on some ego trip or something?"

All the Hebrews had to do, and all we have to do, is follow the Commandments and just "around the corner" to discover the validity and the wisdom of what God wants for us. Let's look at a few ways we can apply God's Second Commandment to our present-day lives.

Recognize Idols for What They Are: Bunk!

In the previous chapter about the First Commandment, we looked at how God forbids the worship or even the acknowledgement of other gods. In this second commandment, He tells us we shouldn't create other gods or likenesses of Him for worship. J. I. Packer writes that the Second Commandment ". . . forbids, not worshipping many gods (the first commandment covered that), but imagining the true God as like yourself or something lower." [1]

This doesn't forbid making images of living things. R. Kent Hughes, an author and the Senior Pastor of College Church in Wheaton, Illinois, explains: "If that were the case, then one has to account for God directing that cherubim be sculpted to preside over the Ark of the Covenant and also be woven into the veil of the Holy of Holies, as well as commanding the embroidery of lilies and pomegranates. Likewise, Solomon's Temple displayed lions, bulls, and cherubim (cf. 1 Kings 7:18–20).

"Rather, what is explicitly forbidden is the making of figures or objects representative of God as objects or aids to worship. It rules out the use of pictorial and sculptured images that depict God as an animal or an object." [2]

Because we can't possibly comprehend God's incredible being, God doesn't want us to use anything to represent Him that would limit our concept of Him. Nothing in physical form adequately represents God, so He tells us not to try. It's too dangerous. It draws our focus away from the truth about Him.

But because God has created us humans with a tremendous need to worship, we tend to want to worship something concrete—something we can handle or see. We are sensual creatures; we have a need to touch, taste, see, smell, and hear. Yet, "God is spirit" (John 4:24) and therefore it takes faith to be content without inanimate objects to represent Him.

It also takes faith to change the mental representations we

create of Him. Karen shared with me her struggle of changing an idol she had fashioned. She writes,

> I created a "false god" whom I thought was the Lord. I based my faith and understanding of Him on this created idol. My god had to function in a way that fit my priorities and be under my control. When my son became ill, I knew it was God's will for him to be instantaneously healed because my image of God was a God who always healed.
>
> But then last year, God began to break apart this box that I had encased Him in. In time, He became the living, true God whom I could allow to reign in my life. Instead of an instantaneous healing for my son, God worked through a long process that actually drew my whole family closer to Him.
>
> We think we know and worship the true God, but usually we serve a god we have created for ourselves that is comfortable for us. We want Him to meet our needs in the way we think best.

When we desire to put a physical or mental concept around our big God, as Karen did, it is an attempt to:

1. Limit God. When we draw, sculpt, or make a form of God in any way, we are drawing boundaries around the God of the Universe who is beyond our comprehension.

2. Control God. If we can limit God, then we can attempt to control Him, to confine Him within the small expectations we believe will work best for our lives. A god made of wood, stone, or pencil can't tell us how to live, can't impose responsibilities, can't require obedience. Such a god can't desire our love. "God" becomes someone who will only ask or require what we're willing to give. John Timmerman wrote, "Idolatry sees God captured and confined in the thing."[3] Such a god is easy to worship and answers our prayers the way we want him to—through our own imaginations.

3. *Fashion God.* If we can create our own image of God, we can also determine the characteristics we want for Him. If we don't want him to be angry with us, we can create a God who is a wimp. If we don't want him to require much from us, we can fashion a God who doesn't have any rules. If we don't want him to say no to us, we can make a god who only says yes to our requests.

We may think we want the kind of God we can limit, control, and fashion, but remember the story of Eve and Satan. Satan hissed that God was trying to withhold something good from Eve, that God wanted to prevent her from becoming a god. If she would disobey Him, she would obtain what she really needed.

Eve's image of God grew smaller as she viewed God as selfish and unloving. In her act of disobedience, Eve tried to replace Almighty God with an idol of her own needs. Her disobedience gave birth to sin because her perceived needs were more important than believing God wanted her good.

You and I do that too when anything becomes more important than God in our lives. That "thing" becomes something we are in charge of. We can limit, control, and fashion it to be who or what we think will make us happy.

Joy Davidman says, "For an idol is not just an image, of one shape or another, meant to represent a deity. An idol is a material object, by the proper manipulation of which [the idolater thinks he] may get what he wants out of life."[4]

Just as Eve's expectations of becoming a god were dashed, so our expectation that a "god" can meet our needs will remain unfulfilled, and may even bring destruction. That's why God in this Second Commandment says, "Don't create gods in physical form or in your mind and expectations. Instead, worship Me in truth." And as we'll find out, He is a God we will want to worship and allow to rule over us.

A Different Kind of Jealousy

It's easy to think God doesn't want to provide for those things we want out of life—like joy and fulfillment—if we don't understand why He refers to His jealousy in conjunction with the Second Commandment: ". . . for I, the Lord your God, am a jealous God."

Jealous? That's such a strong word. It connotes anger and suspicion. We immediately imagine a jealous wife or husband who doubts the motive of everything his or her spouse does. Why did he stay out late after work? Why did she smile at that man in the mall? Why did he give a gift to his secretary? Jealousy, as we normally think of it, is what makes people point accusing fingers, fearful, even terrified that someone else is drawing their beloved away from them.

Unlike us, our all-knowing God knows the truth, He doesn't have to wonder or accuse when it's only a suspicion. He knows our hearts, and like a jealous lover He wants to prevent us from being drawn away by those idols, which will destroy us.

Furthermore, God is the only one who can rightfully demand our devotion. Our spouses cannot. The most our spouses can do is point us to what God says about marriage and say, "Therefore, it is right for you to be faithful to me." But a spouse does not have the *right* to command our faithfulness. That is not a spouse's place.

It's a different story with God. Because God created us and "bought [us] at a price" (1 Corinthians 6:20), He does have the right to demand our devotion. God's jealousy is justified jealousy, whereas human jealousy is ultimately always an attempt to usurp God's position in someone else's life, to make oneself into an idol for another person to worship.

Because of God's love for us, God's jealousy can be described more accurately as "zealousness." In fact the word *jealousy* has its etymological roots in the word *zealous*. Dr. Stuart Briscoe, who is an author and pastor of Elmbrook Church in Brookfield,

Wisconsin, clarifies, "With all the intensity and integrity of His being, He will defend and insist on His rightful place at the center of the universe, on the throne of His creatures' hearts. He will resist with His almighty power anything that infringes on His position." [5]

Our Lord God zealously wants us to remain true to Him. He doesn't want us to serve or worship other gods, or any concept of Him that makes him smaller or less powerful than He really is. He knows that as we make Him Lord and worship only Him, we will be happiest. When other things become idols in our lives, we may initially be happy, but that happiness will wear off because God didn't "program" us to have our spiritual needs met that way. Only He satisfies—just the way He intended.

Alan Redpath writes, "Our maturity, our happiness, our usefulness, are bound up all together with our faithfulness to Him. How anxiously the Lord surveys our actions, thoughts, desires—all because of His tremendous concern for our welfare. God is not jealous *of* us: He is jealous *for* us." [6]

Carolyn realized why God did not want her to make anything or anyone into an idol, not even her husband. Early in her marriage, her anger about her husband's seeming insensitivity built up until she exploded. She says, "At those times, he put his arm around me and listened to an endless list of his shortcomings from his list-maker bride. When I wound down, instead of getting angry in return, Keith calmly apologized for some of his words and actions, clarified others, and held me while I cried on his broad shoulder."

For a time Carolyn's tension dissipated and her love for her husband returned in full force. But not for long. Within a week the tension of unfulfilled expectations overwhelmed her again. She felt like she was on a roller coaster that always crashed in another explosion. What made things worse was her inability to pinpoint what Keith had done to create such monumental disappointment.

At one point of frustration Carolyn turned to Keith in bed. "He was tired, but I needed to talk, needed his advice, needed . . . him. I poked him until, with a groan, he turned over. When he did, I poured out my anger. Oh, I knew it would take time to work things out, but I was too frustrated and angry to care."

For a while Keith listened sleepily. Finally, he interrupted, "Carolyn, who do you go to first with your problems, me . . . or God?"

Carolyn felt as if Keith had slapped her. When he turned over, she steamed, but quietly. In the darkness she looked up and began to see the truth. She explains, "My anger didn't come from anything Keith did. He hadn't changed; I had. Without realizing it, since our marriage I had systematically pushed God off the throne of my life and kept trying to push a very reluctant young husband on. He had become my idol, meant to provide the happiness I craved."

David Seamands, author of *God's Blueprint for Living: New Perspectives on the Ten Commandments*, writes, "The New Testament . . . pictures a jealous God who tolerates no rival for the throne of our hearts. God has enemies, yes, but no rivals."[7]

The Benefits of Obeying God

God's zeal for our good is what causes Him to go to great lengths to keep us unhindered by false gods. In the next part of the commandment he says he will punish the children for the sin of the fathers to the third and fourth generation of those who hate Him, but show love to a thousand generations of those who love Him and keep His commandments.

We can often see God's preset consequences for wrong behavior in the children of people who set up idols for themselves such as alcoholism, drug addiction, anger, and many other kinds of "gods." Although this is not true in every case, the habitual sins of parents are often passed along, either genetically or through influence and example. God has put into place a spiritual law that says parents will influence their children for good or for evil. Yet, people are still responsible for their own choices.

In contrast, there is a blessing for those who choose God's way. God will show love to a thousand generations of those who love Him and keep His commandments. In His amazing grace, God's discipline will only be for a few short generations, but His love and reward will extend much longer to the families and descendants of those who seek Him.

God loves to reward obedience, and even if just one person in a family turns from generational disobedience toward God, He will respond in love, mercy, and grace to that person and their descendants.

What rewards can we count on? Here are just a few:

- peace (Isaiah 48:18)
- knowledge of being a child of God (Jeremiah 7:23)
- prolonged life (Deuteronomy 5:32–33)
- power when we're tempted (1 Corinthians 10:13)
- righteousness (Romans 6:16).
- sanctification (1 Peter 1:2).

Our God is a generous God!

Ministry as an Idol

If we don't have the correct perspective about God's love, mercy, and grace, we will be more tempted to worship that which can't really meet our needs. Even good things can become idols. Dr. Stuart Briscoe tells in his book, *Playing by the Rules*, about the time his ministry—something good in itself—became an idol.

God had been opening wonderful new doors of opportunity for Dr. Briscoe. It was exciting, until Briscoe suffered from an illness that prevented him from ministering at all. He felt depressed, unable to fulfill those great opportunities. He says, "My concern, I told myself, stemmed from the fact that I loved to preach about the Lord Jesus. Then in my own heart God spoke to me powerfully, saying 'Stuart Briscoe, do you love preaching about the Lord Jesus more than you love the Lord Jesus about whom you preach?' The answer was yes. I knew I felt upset with the Lord Jesus because I could not preach about Him."

Dr. Briscoe realized that if he had really been excited about *Jesus*, not about *preaching about Jesus*, whether or not he could preach wouldn't have mattered. He began to correct his perspective and give up his idol of preaching. He again turned to Jesus to be the focus of his life. As a result, God again made it possible for him to preach.

Briscoe says, "When a good thing becomes overimportant to us, it becomes our possession. We get so excited about it that we worship ourselves rather than the Lord, as in the case of my ministry, which had turned into idolatry; that sin destroyed its effectiveness." [8]

Dr. Briscoe's experience can be like ours to one degree or another. Anything that becomes more important than Jesus is the thing we are worshiping.

J. I. Packer wrote, ". . . the positive purpose of the second commandment becomes plain. Negatively, it is a warning against ways of worship and religious practice that lead us to dishonor God and to falsify His truth. Positively, it is a summons to us to recognise that God the Creator is transcendent, mysterious, and inscrutable, beyond the range of any imagining or philosophical guesswork of which we are capable." [9]

Parental Influence

One of the primary ways we absorb our ideas about God comes from the way we were raised. Listen to the accounts of three people who formed wrong ideas about God because of negative parental influences.

Anita says,

I used to have the idea that God the Father was too harsh to approach. I believed He was looking for the wrong things I did so that He could punish me, even though I read in the Bible that He is love. Where the Bible states to fear God, I literally did so. I didn't see God as lovable until I dealt with the childhood abuse I received from my father. Completely unaware of what was happening, I had transferred my image of my earthly father to God the Father in heaven. As I dealt with memories of abuse from my father and my defenses against the abuse, there was room inside of me to view my father in a different way and my Heavenly Father as well.

Stan says, "When I was a child and was naughty, my mother would wag her finger in my face and tell me that God would punish me for being naughty. My fear of God was real fear, not reverence. In time I totally abandoned God because I could never measure up to the expectations I thought He had of me. Many years later, I learned that 'fear' as we read in the Bible really means respect and honor. It was then I could begin to view my Heavenly Father as a loving God."

Dianne writes, "The biggest wrong idea about God I had was a God of wrath and anger like my earthly father. Learning about God's love for me and accepting it was difficult since I had not seen it displayed through other people. The only way to correct it was to study His word and make a decision to believe His word by faith. The difference was like the difference between night and day, light and dark, love and fear, and life and death. I could never have served a God that instilled only fear in me. I needed to know Him as a God of love."

Anita, Stan, and Dianne are grateful God wanted them to know the truth about Him. As they corrected their perceptions about God, they were set free from the idols of fear and terror. God wants each of us to have that same freedom from idols that wear a mask, pretending to be God yet keeping us at a distance from His wonderful love.

Jesus: the Very Face of God

If you or I were to query a group of people with the question, "How do you describe God?" we would receive a wide variety of answers. But the person who gave the answer, "God's best description is Jesus," would have the right answer.

William Law wisely wrote, "The attributes we give God are only human ways of coming to grips with a vastness that is beyond our metaphors and terminology." [10]

Although describing God through His attributes is inadequate, it is an effective way of getting some "grip" upon God's vastness. We can rightly do that by observing Jesus' life.

Colossians 1:15–19 tells us,

[Jesus] is the image of the invisible God, the firstborn over all creation. For by him all things were created: things in heaven and on earth, visible and invisible, whether thrones or powers or rulers or authorities; all things were created by him and for him. He is before all things, and in him all things hold together. And he is the head of the body, the church; he is the beginning and the firstborn from among the dead, so that in everything he might have the supremacy. For God was pleased to have all his fullness dwell in him, and through him to reconcile to himself all things, whether things on earth or things in heaven, by making peace through his blood, shed on the cross.

J. I. Packer writes, "How should we form thoughts of God? Not only can we not imagine him adequately, since he is at every point greater than we can grasp; we dare not trust anything our imagination suggests about him, for the built-in habit of fallen minds is to scale God down . . . He has made a point of showing us both his hand and his heart, in his words and deeds recorded in Scripture, and supremely in the earthly life of his incarnate Son, Jesus Christ, who is in every sense his image." [11]

David Seamands writes, ". . . look at the face of Jesus Christ. The only true picture of God is in his face . . . Methodist missionary E. Stanley Jones said, 'You and I know almost nothing about God except what we see in Jesus Christ, and most of the little we do know is wrong.'" [12]

Our Father wants us to know Him through His Son Jesus. Theologian C. H. Spurgeon wrote, "The highest science, the loftiest speculation, the mightiest philosophy, which can ever engage the attention of a child of God, is the name, the nature, the person, the work, the doings, and the existence of the great God whom [Jesus] calls his Father." [13]

As we read about Jesus' life in the Gospel accounts, we see the Heavenly Father and the personality of the Trinity reflected. As a result, we can see the following attributes of God:

- **love**: Jesus lovingly and willingly hung on the cross, sacrificing His own life in a dreadful manner of death so that He could reconcile sinful humans to His Father. (Mark 15:38)

- **compassion and forgiveness**: Jesus treated the woman caught in adultery in a compassionate, tender manner, and forgave her of her immoral sin. (John 8:1–11)

- **wrath**: Jesus cleansed the Temple of the unrighteous selling of sacrificial animals for profit. (John 2:13–25)

I could continue forever describing Jesus' attributes of holiness, wisdom, grace, justice, goodness, and on and on. There are not enough words to describe all that our great God is, and we see each quality demonstrated in Jesus.

As we develop awareness of and appreciation for God's attributes, we will not have a need to create idols, which make God seem smaller than He is. Instead, we'll experience the truth of knowing the greatness of the true and living God.

Releasing Control

One of the best ways we can follow the Second Commandment is to resist the temptation to be in charge of life (and that includes controlling others). We must allow God to be God.

Theologian A. W. Tozer writes, "Left to ourselves we tend immediately to reduce God to manageable terms. We want to get Him where we can use Him, or at least know where He is when we need Him. We want a God we can in some measure control." [14]

When we try to control God, it is revealed in striking ways:

- We try to use the idol of anger to make our significant other do what we want him or her to do.
- We fret with the idol of worry about the past and the future.
- We focus on the idol of figuring out why God is allowing a certain difficulty in our lives, so that we can convince Him we really don't need to be disciplined in such a way.
- We dangle the idol of our tithe before God's face with the wrong motive of obtaining financial security.
- We allow the idols of bitterness and resentment to corrode our emotions because we don't want the person who hurt us to be released from punishment.
- We incorporate the idol of gossip as a way to tear others down and thus build ourselves up in the minds of others.

We may think that all these ways of "coping" are gaining us the love, peace, joy, and fulfillment we desire, but as Stuart Briscoe says, "Idolatry places man in control of God, but at a terrible price. Isaiah describes what had happened to his people this way, 'Your idols have become a burden to you.'"[15]

Pastor Roger Barrier describes how the burden of idolatry affected him.

I am cursed with a runaway mind. Some call me a worry-wart. Others brand me as overly anxious. I'm constantly burdened with the idol of, 'What if?'

One Saturday night I found myself sitting in tears behind the couch in our den. Sunday morning sermons were fast approaching, and I was in no shape to preach. Something was wrong. My emotions were frayed. I had four ulcers. I had high blood pressure. After crying out for help, I learned some anxiety-prevention techniques that put God back at the control center of my life and thinking.

We live in a society of frantic activity. Pastors often seem to be the most hurried, harried people I know. Seventy work hours per week were normal for me when I began pastoring. My fatigue—and worry—increased daily. My near collapse showed me my pace could not last forever. Fortunately, I had wise leaders who helped slow me down.

As my pace slowed, my overactive mind slowed, too. My runaway thoughts were easier to corral. Worry was no longer my idol.[16]

We also practice idolatry when we try to dictate the terms by which God will work in our lives. Melinda describes how a woman asked her pastor-husband, "Rev. Fish, will you pray over my lottery tickets and bless them for me? The Lord wants me to have a ministry, and this is how He's going to provide."

We may laugh at such a ludicrous example and think we would never craft an idol like that, but we can still do it in other, more subtle ways. How can we know whether we are using our own selfishly motivated and false ideas about God to carve an idol? Stacey Padrick suggests asking ourselves these questions:

- What often preoccupies or rules my heart? thoughts? time?
- What often compels me? controls me? drives me? motivates me?
- To what does my heart cling? To what might I be overattached?
- What often competes for my time with God? my spouse? my family?
- What gives me a sense of worth? What defines me before others?
- What do I crave?
- If everything else were taken away, what is one thing I could not bear to live without?
- Am I looking to something or someone to provide what only God truly can?
- What do family or close friends think may be idols in my life? [17]

As we evaluate our motives, desires, and priorities, we may see clues about the idols we are fashioning. In addition, we can ask ourselves, "What do I feel tense about at the thought of losing?" When you come up with that answer, make a conscious choice to release it into God's hands. Stacey Padrick suggests "fasting" from whatever holds the place of an idol in your heart.

If your idol is trying to change your husband, can you fast from telling him how to do something the next time you feel compelled to? Instead, focus on God's sovereignty. He is in control and is much more effective at changing someone from the inside. He is also much better at knowing when change is necessary.

If your idol is anxiety about your child driving at night, can you fast from dwelling on the potential dangers and pray for his or her safety instead? Focus on God's attribute of power because He is able to protect your child even more than if you were driving the car.

If your idol is the belief that there is only one way God can answer your prayer for the healing of a beloved family member, can you fast from your expectations and thank God that He will do the right thing for that person, you, and the whole universe? Focus on God's love. He not only knows what's best in His wisdom; in His love He will make sure it comes to pass.

As you and I expose our idols to God's light of truth, and then smash them with the truth of God's wonderful nature, we will experience the blessings of God's love in our lives and in the lives of our descendants, as He promised in the Second Commandment. As we do that, we'll join Russell in saying, "My purpose in life is learning that He is God, not I."

Search Yourself

Why do people create physical and mental idols?

⁓✺⁓

Do you find the idea of God's "jealousy" favorable or frightening? How do you think God wants you to view it? How can you change your perspective to coincide with God's perspective?

⁓✺⁓

Is there something in your life that in itself is good but that has become an idol? If so, what does God want you to do about it?

⁓✺⁓

What in the Gospel accounts of Jesus represents the most important attribute of God to you?

⁓✺⁓

Are you practicing idolatry by trying to control your life or the lives of others? What will you do to release control and trust God?

A *name* is *a kind of face*
whereby one is known.

THOMAS FULLER

RULE
III

Give God the Respect He Deserves

YOU SHALL NOT MISUSE THE NAME OF THE LORD YOUR
GOD, FOR THE LORD WILL NOT HOLD ANYONE GUILT-
LESS WHO MISUSES HIS NAME.

EXODUS 20:7

Carrie and Tim had adopted a little girl and were thrilled
to have a new baby in the family. A year later, the social
worker called to say that their adopted daughter's birth
mother was putting her other child, a four-year-old boy
named Johnny, up for adoption. She asked, "Would you
be willing to adopt him also?"

Carrie and Tim wondered about the complications of
welcoming an older child into their home but eventually
agreed to having Johnny visit on a try-it-and-see basis.

For several months Johnny visited on weekends and
then began spending more time with Carrie and Tim.
Soon they were ready to welcome Johnny into the family.

After Tim explained to Johnny that he was about to become their legitimate son, Johnny was excited and exclaimed, "When I come here to live all the time, I want *my* name to be Tim!"

His father-to-be was perplexed. He tried to convince Johnny how special his own name was because that was the name his birth mother had given him.

"No, Tim, I want your name."

"But, Johnny," the man tried again, "it would be too confusing for both of us to have the same name."

The boy spoke up quickly. "But I can use your name because you won't need it anymore."

"Why not? I've always needed it in the past."

"Because when I come here to live all the time, your name will be Daddy."

Names are powerful! God wants us to lovingly and reverently call *Him* Daddy, but in order to do that we must resist the temptation to misuse His name, or even use it lightly. That's the message of the Third Commandment. God's name is serious business and we must regard and treat it with the utmost respect and reverence. As David Seamands puts it, "The person who learns true reverence knows God's name is the doorway to the audience chamber of the Lord."[1] If we do learn and practice true reverence, we can be assured that God will brag about us the same way he did Levi, one of his first priests: ". . . he revered me and stood in awe of my name" (Malachi 2:5).

God's Name

In America we don't look at names the same way people did in ancient Jewish culture. Names in our society are with few exceptions arbitrary labels of convenience. Rarely does anything more than sound or novelty determine what we name our children. Even when we say a name has meaning, we are usually not referring to the same sort of meaning the ancient Hebrews were. When we say little Joey is named after his grandfather Joe and that therefore the name Joey really is meaningful, we are saying something quite different than what Jesus meant, for example, when he gave Simon the name Peter (John 1:42). In biblical times, a name was an expression or an extension of the name-bearer. Names were more like our present-day nicknames (e.g., Grumpy, Sugar, or Silly) than our proper names (e.g., Tom or Jennifer).

With this in mind, let's look at how Moses stated one of his concerns to God when God appeared to him in the burning bush: "Suppose I go to the Israelites and say to them, 'The God of your fathers has sent me to you,' and they ask me, 'What is his name?' Then what shall I tell them?" (Exodus 3:13).

God replies, "I AM WHO I AM. This is what you are to say to the Israelites: 'I AM has sent me to you'" (Exodus 3:14).

There were a lot of gods in those days, as mentioned before, and Moses knew that the Israelites would want to know which one had appeared to him. Knowing gods' names was a way of distinguishing one from another. When God replied, "I am who I am," He was saying several things:

- "I am that I am."
- "I am what I do."
- "I cause to become."
- "I shall be as I shall be."
- "I am who I am."

But the main concept He wanted to convey was His eternal existence. "I am." Whereas the many gods of Egypt could come and go, the Almighty God of the Hebrews existed forever and never changed. Whereas men had named the idol gods when they formed them, this God had named Himself.

Well-known Christian writer Liz Curtis Higgs writes, "But God really is everlasting. That means he will still be around when the universe isn't.

"I can, in my own limited way, grasp the idea of forever going forward through time . . . somewhere out there, infinity, forever and ever, amen. But if God is everlasting, he also goes all the way back! Backward not only through time, but before time, a constraint he created for his convenience and ours.

"God is, was, and always will be. And all without a nap."[2]

God's act of allowing His greatness to be named, so that people could put a label on Him, is a demonstration of His desire for us to know Him. A name is the very first distinction between someone we call a stranger and someone we call a friend.

Stuart Briscoe comments, "When God revealed His name, He took the initiative, saying, 'Man, you can't make Me the way you want Me to be. I am. As the "I am" I will demonstrate who I am, so that you will have no questions about it.' . . . When God introduces Himself to Abraham or Moses or anyone else, in effect He says, 'I'm knowable. I want to introduce Myself to you.'"[3]

In spite of God's overture, we must still regard Him with awe and deference. That's why the Third Commandment is so important. God is telling us, "Yes, I'm knowable, but we aren't on the same level. I am still the Lord God Almighty."

The Jews took this reverence to an extreme, as demonstrated when a scribe was to write the name of God. Such a scribe would first bathe and don full Jewish dress before he would dip his pen in ink. Once he started writing that sacred name, he refused any and all interruptions, even the call of a king.

God's name was considered so sacred and holy that it was only spoken one time a year by the High Priest in the Holy of Holies on the Day of Atonement (Yom Kippur). Because of the limited use of the spoken name of God, its pronunciation has been lost forever.

Moreover, the vowels of the name were not written and so, over the years, similar to the spoken name of God, those vowels have been forgotten. As a result, we cannot write it correctly but have taken the word "YHWH" to designate the Lord God.

God did not command such limits on His spoken or written name. The above-mentioned losses are the result of oral traditions determined by Jewish priests of long ago. I doubt God intended for His name to be treated that way. If God wants us to talk to Him, and He does, He probably wants us to call Him by His self-designated name. Thankfully, if we sincerely call upon Him, He will acknowledge us no matter what name we use, because He loves us.

His love was revealed in the person of Jesus, who came onto the human scene and spoke freely in the name of the Father he loved. Jesus himself told us the attitude we should have when addressing God. In Matthew 6:9 Jesus instructed His followers how to pray: "Our Father in heaven, hallowed be your name . . ." The word *hallowed* means holy and set apart. It refers to the opposite of something common. Jesus was encouraging us to keep the name of God lifted high in value and opinion, the very same thing the Third Commandment is telling us to do.

Take a Vow

The Third Commandment tells us not to misuse God's name. Today's English Version says it this way: "Do not use my name for evil purposes." God warns us that if we use His name for evil purposes, we will be held accountable at great cost.

The King James translates the Hebrew, "Thou shalt not take the name of the Lord thy God in vain." We can understand the word *vain* by looking at its related word *vanity*. John H. Timmerman writes, "A vanity is any attempt to see divine mysteries exclusively in human terms. . . any attempt to humanize the divine is a vanity, an emptiness. In fact, our word 'vain' derives from the Latin *vanus*: empty. When we use the name of God simply for human purposes, apart from a sense of worship and awe, we are emptying the majesty of God."[4]

That is why taking a vow is not wrong in itself. If it is done with the right motives, for the right thing, and the vow is kept in God's power, a vow can be a way of solidifying our good commitments. When we get married we take a vow to be loyal. When we take a vow in court, we commit to tell the truth. Those are right and necessary things, but God through the Third Commandment is referring to those vows that are used incorrectly and with wrong motives—and that bring dishonor to His holy name.

God's Word gives requirements for such vows. Deuteronomy 10:20 tells us, "Fear the Lord your God and serve him. Hold fast to him and take your oaths in his name." God allowed this so people would have a way of saying they intended to do as they promised. Originally, such oaths were ways of saying things like, "I will repay my loan to you because God knows everything and will punish me if I don't," or "I will keep my promise because God has heard me make it." But over time, people began to use such vows casually. They didn't keep their promises.

Billy Graham writes, "I remember when I was a boy on a small farm in North Carolina, a man's word was as good as his bond. I seriously doubt if my father ever signed a contract in the many deals he made for cows, horses, mules, and machinery. A handshake was enough. Today you have to employ lawyers to draw up the most intricate and complex contracts, and even they do not provide a complete safeguard against the fraud, cheating, and lying so prevalent today."[5]

Today, not only are vows—even those sworn to with God's name—not kept; God's name is used in contemptuous and careless ways. Unlike the Jews who carefully refrained from using God's name at all, we have gone to the other but equally wrong extreme. Today, the word *God* is used all the time, but it is rarely used to refer to God Himself.

A Lesson from Job

We can learn a lot about giving God the respect He deserves by studying Job. When Job and his wife were attacked by Satan, and their family and possessions were destroyed, Job's wife was at the end of her rope.

She said to Job, "Are you still holding on to your integrity? Curse God and die!" (Job 2:9). Apparently, Job's wife wanted Job to curse God, so that God would strike him dead, ending his agony.

But Job stayed true and replied, "You are talking like a foolish woman. Shall we accept good from God, and not trouble?"

Job believed God had allowed his trials but did not believe God was doing something wrong, no matter how much suffering it caused. Consider that Job was suffering as much as or more than anyone in history and you begin to see just how faithful he was to God. He was a keeper of the Third Commandment.

As Job was, you and I need to be careful not to attribute evil to God. When God has allowed us to experience trials and difficulties, it's appropriate for us to ask why, but it is sin to conclude from our trials that God doesn't know what He's doing. That makes God smaller than He is.

Selfishness: The Lousy Leader

Another way of misusing God's name is prompted by selfishness. In politics, we constantly see the selfish use of God's name. As the presidential campaign gears up, politicians who sense Americans' interest in integrity and values suddenly start mentioning religion, the Bible, and God in their speeches. If God is popular, they believe in Him. If He's not on the top of the polls, they leave Him out.

I recently read an interview in the newspaper about Suze Orman, the best-selling author of *The Courage to Be Rich*, a book that links wealth with spirituality. In a speaking engagement, Ms. Orman tells a woman, "Your new truth should be: 'I have more money than I'll ever need.' You know what I think happens? God looks down and says, 'I better make that come true!'"[6] Orman's book preaches the "good news" that God will do whatever we want Him to do.

But before we point our fingers at peddlers of prosperity, we would do well to notice another selfishly motivated misuse of God's name, which we Christians practice frequently. We often claim to know God's will without so much as whispering a prayer.

John H. Timmerman wrote, "It is human vanity to think one knows everything about God; our knowledge apart from God's revelation is a comparative emptiness."[7]

Karen says, "God has been teaching me that we take His name in vain when we pray without knowing or asking His will. We pray "in Jesus' name" at the end of our prayers, but have we prayed it in His name or our name?

"Lately I have been asking God how He wants me to pray for someone or something before I begin. It's amazing how different His perspective is from mine. He may be allowing pain in a friend's life for the purpose of strengthening him or her, and all I want is for my friend (and me!) to be out of misery."

Robin tells about her first year out of college. In the span of a year three different Christian men told her, "The Lord has told me we are going to get married." Not only did Robin not want to marry any of them, she hadn't heard the same word from God! These men were being presumptuous and were misusing God's name.

A third way we misuse God's name is through insincerity. Jesus referred to this form of vain usage when He said, "Not everyone who says to me, 'Lord, Lord,' will enter the kingdom of heaven, but only he who does the will of my Father who is in heaven. Many will say to me on that day, 'Lord, Lord, did we not prophesy in your name, and in your name drive out demons and perform many miracles?' Then I will tell them plainly, 'I never knew you. Away from me, you evildoers!'" (Matthew 7:21–23).

The people Jesus refers to may have said the words, 'Lord, Lord,' but they hadn't made God the Master of their lives. This kind of "empty God-speak" would be similar to confessing a sin with no intention of refraining from it or testing God by doing something foolish and then praying we don't suffer the consequences. A promiscuous woman prays she won't get pregnant or become infected with disease. We drive over the speed limit and then pray there are no policemen watching.

Sometimes people use God's name merely for effect, as when someone says, "What in God's name are you doing?" or "God, have I got a headache." But would you use silk for toilet paper? Would you use a priceless china plate for a frisbee? Some things are simply too valuable to be used for cheap purposes; God's name is one of them.

I used the phrase "God bless you" some time ago but realized later it wasn't appropriate. I attended the funeral of a teenager who had committed suicide and the family didn't know the Lord personally. In an effort to comfort the deceased boy's mother I said "God bless you" to her. She looked at me quizzically but didn't respond.

Although I sincerely meant God wanted to use this situation for good in her life, I understood later that she wasn't in any state of mind to see God's hand of blessing and most likely thought her pain was His curse. It would have been better to love her through sharing in the silence of her grief. God's name should be used to bless and not curse. We need to make sure it will be received that way.

We can do injustice to God's name by giving information about God or His will that is incorrect—even if we have the best intentions. I fell into that temptation when I talked with my friend Linda as she battled cancer. We went to high school together, and I knew she was a Christian. When I heard she had cancer, I called her in the hospital. She sounded weak and discouraged. Our conversation led to her question, "You don't think it's God's will for me to die, do you?"

My mind was paralyzed. What should I say? I didn't really know her condition, yet I didn't want to discourage her. In that moment of confusion, I blurted out, "Why, of course not! I'm sure you're going to be fine." That seemed to relieve her and we talked further. Then I promised to call again and said goodbye.

What had I done? I didn't know God's will for her! Why hadn't I just said I didn't know? I mentally kicked myself and couldn't find the courage to call her back again. Several weeks later she died. I was crushed to think I had misled her and misrepresented the Lord. I had misused His name. I had also not kept my promise to call her back.

Selfishness distorts our perspective of who God is and thereby leads us to misuse His name in many different ways.

God's Many Names

Each of the "gods" that the Lord God wanted the Israelites to resist had one name and therefore only one characteristic. One god was in charge of agriculture, another was in charge of rain. Each puny, man-made god was limited in its abilities and power. But our God has many names or titles, each one pointing to a different characteristic, and they are all good.

My friend Joan expresses the sentiment of many Christians who have studied God's names: "I love the different names of God. There is a name for every circumstance. I love the sound of them. They are filled with such majesty and royalty. Those names are precious to me." The more His names are precious to us, the more we'll desire to see His name lifted and given the credit it deserves. Here are a few names for us to consider.

Adonai, Lord: This name refers to God's position as Master over our lives. Kay Arthur writes, "The lordship of God means His total possession of me and my total submission to Him as Lord and Master."[8] When we call God our Lord, Adonai, we are saying we will obey His commands and follow His leading.

Abba, Father: God wants us to know Him as our "Daddy." Just like Johnny, in the opening story, we each long to have a relationship with God who will be the perfect Father. Kurt shared with me, "The most profound of God's names for me has been 'Abba.' The idea of being God's child and His adopted son was never explained to me. Instead, I had always considered myself His slave, His serf. When 'Abba' was translated for me as 'Papa,' I knew I could approach Him. I understood for the first time that everything from Him was meant in love and given especially to me as His chosen offspring."

Jehovah-Shammah, The Lord Is There: God is everywhere and always with us. He is omnipresent and always available. But developing an ability to sense His presence can be difficult. Brother Lawrence (1611–1691), a French mystic, wrote,

> I worshiped him as frequently as I could, keeping my mind in his holy presence and calling my attention back to him when it wandered.

This wasn't easy, but I kept at it. I made this my business all day long, not just at special prayer times. At all times, every hour, every minute, even in the height of my business, I drove away from my mind everything that was capable of interrupting my thoughts of God. Although I have not been entirely successful at this, I have still found great advantage in it.[9]

Jehovah Shalom, The Lord Is Peace: Whenever we are afraid, we can call upon the God who is in charge of everything and wants only our best.

Elaine realized she hadn't been doing that. She was returning home from a trip with her husband, her pastor, and her pastor's wife. Her pastor was driving sensibly, but dark clouds, a strong wind, and dropping temperatures warned of a possible storm. They approached a flat stretch of road in Missouri, known to be dangerous, where the wind always whistled across the flats. It began to sleet.

Suddenly Elaine's fears overwhelmed her, and almost screaming she said, "I can't stand it, we have to stop. Get off at that exit." The pastor's wife turned around and touched her hand. "Elaine, have faith! God is with us."

Elaine remembers how embarrassed she was. "I discovered faith and fear are the flip sides of each other. I learned that fear likes to be in charge. I was placing fear higher than my faith in God. For many years I was willing to alter my life according to my fear. So I began to fight fear instead of giving in to it."

There are so many other wonderful names of God. Have you studied them? You might want to consider books like *Lord, I Want To Know You* by Kay Arthur (Multnomah). Also, I have written a Bible study entitled *Character of the King*, which is about the qualities of God. By reflecting on the many names of God, we will learn more about who He is, and giving Him the respect He deserves will come naturally.

Search Yourself

When you think of God's name being "misused,"
what do you think of?

❧

What can we learn from Job about keeping the
Third Commandment?

❧

How have you found yourself misusing God's
name for selfish purposes?

❧

When you think of the various names of God,
which one is most important to you and why?

O day most calm,

most bright,

The fruit of this,

the next world's bud.

GEORGE HERBERT

RULE IV

Enjoy God's Gift of Time

REMEMBER THE SABBATH DAY BY KEEPING IT HOLY. SIX
DAYS YOU SHALL LABOR AND DO ALL YOUR WORK,
BUT THE SEVENTH DAY IS A SABBATH TO THE LORD
YOUR GOD. ON IT YOU SHALL NOT DO ANY WORK,
NEITHER YOU, NOR YOUR SON OR DAUGHTER, NOR
YOUR MANSERVANT OR MAIDSERVANT, NOR YOUR
ANIMALS, NOR THE ALIEN WITHIN YOUR GATES. FOR IN
SIX DAYS THE LORD MADE THE HEAVENS AND THE
EARTH, THE SEA, AND ALL THAT IS IN THEM, BUT HE
RESTED ON THE SEVENTH DAY. THEREFORE THE LORD
BLESSED THE SABBATH DAY
AND MADE IT HOLY.

EXODUS 20:8-11

Recently I heard about a devout Baptist family, living in
Pinehurst, Washington, who in the early 1950s had a very
peculiar way of observing the Sabbath.

Where the King James Version refers to the Sabbath as
a "solemn assembly" in Leviticus 23:36, this family took
it to mean they should stay home and not attend worship

services. The family prepared their three Sunday meals on Saturday from foods that could be left on the table overnight. Sunday clothes were laid out in order to minimize commotion. After rising and dressing, the entire family—husband, wife, and two kids—would sit in a row on the living room couch from morning until evening with hands folded silently. The two children were required to sit erect, propped between the parents in case either should happen to nap. They answered neither door nor phone. No one could speak, except to excuse oneself to use the bathroom, and whoever did was sure to come right back to the appropriate seat.

Fortunately, I doubt this family's commitment is what God had in mind when He gave the next commandment we'll consider. God is a God of celebration and festivity. He is not dour. The Israelites' legalism led them to attach additional rules to God's commandment, but God's desire was for His people to set aside a day to rest, and to remember all that He had done in their lives.

Remember

God's first word in this commandment is "remember," and the Israelites had much to remember. First, as is mentioned in Exodus 20:8–11, they needed to remember that God created the world in six days and rested on the seventh. But why did God rest? Was He tired? Of course not. God doesn't expend energy at all when He works. No, He stopped because He was satisfied with what He had done.

We would find greater satisfaction in our work if we followed God's lead. He worked hard for six days, but on the seventh day, God put away His tools, hung up His apron, clapped the dust off his hands, and pronounced it all "good." He set aside a whole day to sit back and just "soak it in." What joy we'd find if we did the same.

Second, God's people would have done well to remember that they had been delivered from Egyptian slavery. When they worked for those browbeating taskmasters, they didn't have *any* days off, but God wanted what was good for them and that included a day off. What a contrast to those Egyptians! Not only would a day of rest give the Israelites a chance to relax, it would provide a special opportunity for them to remember His deliverance and power.

That is what God wants us to do also. If we don't stop our frenzied activity, we can't reflect on all that God has done for us. We just keep looking to the future and all that still needs to be done. Instead, we should stop, look backward for a moment, and, for example, give thanks for His help with that project we doubted we could finish. Or perhaps we should recognize how we've been more patient with the kids because we have been seeking His will. Or maybe we should contemplate how this past week He answered a prayer we've been saying for several years. Without a Sabbath rest, we won't stop to remember what God has done for us.

Third, some of the Israelites would have remembered that just one week before God gave them the Fourth Commandment, He had provided them with manna—food for their nourishment. We too need to remember how God provides for our day-to-day needs. Food. Shelter. Friends. Family. We won't remember to thank God for these things unless we set aside a day to do so. God told the Israelites and now He tells us, "Stop, drop, and roll your mind over the evidence of My faithfulness."

Jesus: The New Way

As time went along, the blessing that God desired for His people turned into a legalistic litany of dos and don'ts that burdened the people instead of setting them free. As people tried to understand and follow God's rule, they came to the priests and asked whether doing a certain thing was considered work. "Hmmm," the priests murmured as they put their heads together.

By the time Jesus was born, the Jewish priests had compiled the Mishna, which listed no less than 1,521 things to avoid. Because people had a difficult time remembering that many rules, a whole division of rabbis were hired and trained to teach the Mishna. Here's a sampling of the Mishna's rules:

- No traveling more than 1,000 yards
- No plucking gray hair; that's work
- No cooking
- No tearing of paper, wrappers, etc.
- No handling of money
- No writing
- No cutting hair or nails
- No gardening

Did God intend such extremes? Of course not. But we humans are good at taking God's simple, loving rules and turning them into burdens.

Well-known Christian writer Max Lucado tells us to examine legalism closely. "Something is missing," he says. "What is it? Joy. What's there? Fear. (That you won't do enough.) Arrogance. (That you have done enough). Failure. (That you have made a mistake.)

"Legalism is a dark world."[1]

Instead of fearing we're not observing the Sabbath correctly, we can feel free to follow God's individual call upon our lives within the guidelines given in the New Testament.

In Matthew 12:1–8, when Jesus and his disciples walked through a grainfield on a Sabbath and ate some grain, the Pharisees accused them of "working." Jesus corrected the Pharisees by reminding them of the time David ate consecreated bread. He pointed out the fact that priests worked on the Sabbath in their worship services. Jesus let them know that he and his disciples were working for God and that therefore they were in the right.

Jesus continued time and again to shake the priests and rabbis up by doing such forbidden things as healing on the Sabbath. He was setting his people free from unintended restrictions. "The Sabbath was made for man, not man for the Sabbath," he said (Mark 2:27–28).

Interestingly, the Fourth Commandment is the only commandment not specifically repeated in the New Testament as a requirement for Christian obedience, although the early church at the Jerusalem council in Acts 15:19–31 did tell the new converts to "obey the law of Moses" (Acts 15:5). Over time the new church began to meet not on Saturday, the official Jewish Sabbath, but on Sunday because Jesus rose from the dead on the first day of the week.

To this day, some groups of Christians continue to celebrate the Sabbath on the seventh day and that is fine. Paul wrote, "Therefore do not let anyone judge you by what you eat or drink, or with regard to a religious festival, a New Moon celebration or a Sabbath day. These are a shadow of the things that were to come; the reality, however, is found in Christ" (Colossians 2:16–17). Which day we choose to observe the Sabbath is not the important thing. The important thing is that we obey God's commandment to take one day a week to rest and focus on Him.

$\mathcal{A}$ $\mathcal{D}ay$ with a $\mathcal{B}ow$ on $\mathcal{T}op$

Poet Samuel Taylor Coleridge said, "I feel as if God had, by giving the Sabbath, given fifty-two springs in every year." The Sabbath is truly a gift from God for His people.

I've seen the gift of this commandment in my own life. Awhile ago, though I may have taken a nap on Sunday afternoons after church, I began to use Sunday as a time to complete some writing projects, especially if a deadline was approaching.

Then, several years ago, the Lord started to convict me about setting aside a Sabbath rest. After making the decision to observe the Sabbath, initially I could barely stay away from my office, which is located in my home. But as I did, more and more I felt a deep sense of spiritual, physical, and emotional rest. As I attended church and then took time to focus on the Lord as our family spent the afternoon together, I was amazed to find that everything God really wanted me to do in my work was done—even though I didn't work on Sundays.

Psalm 127:1–2 took on new meaning for me. "Unless the Lord builds the house, its builders labor in vain. Unless the Lord watches over the city, the watchmen stand guard in vain. In vain you rise early and stay up late, toiling for food to eat— for he grants sleep to those he loves." I realized that I was trying to build the "house" (my ministry) in my own power and God wanted me to do it in His. Refraining from work on Sundays became the way I allowed Him to "watch the city," to be Lord even over my work.

Because I speak at women's retreats that often require me to speak or travel on Sundays, I've made another day of the week my Sabbath, and God has honored it. I can't say I've kept this commitment perfectly, but the vast majority of the time I do.

The peace and serenity I've found as a result is, I believe, what God wanted us to experience. Dr. Laura Schlessinger writes, "If life is like a downhill bike ride in which speed increases and becomes increasingly difficult to stop, then Sabbaths are regularly scheduled stop signs that bring us to a halt, making time pass a little bit slower so that we might appreciate it more."[2]

For the Israelites traveling toward the Promised Land who had the stress of surviving in the wilderness, or for modern Americans who have the stress of surviving in a different but equally challenging wilderness (because it *is* a jungle out there), the keeping of the Sabbath is God's stop sign for the restoration of our spirits and the rest of our bodies.

If we will just face the reality of God's created order and pay attention to the needs of our bodies, we will gladly give in to the gift of the Sabbath. David A. Seamands writes, "One of the basic principles of personality, whether the divine or the human, is the need for rhythmic alteration between work and rest. God worked creatively for six days, then He rested for the seventh. This Fourth Commandment is not only written on tablets of stone but also on the tablets of our hearts, our bodies, our emotions and our minds. This law is written into every cell of the human body."[3]

Just consider the rhythms all around us: high and low tide, day turning into night, the seasons, sowing and harvesting, the hibernation of many animals. When we allow ourselves to rest, we are cooperating with God's grand scheme for health and rejuvenation. When we don't, we are working contrary to the Engineer's *User's Manual,* so to speak, and are likely to develop "stress fractures."

J. I. Packer encourages us to think of it this way:

"Satan wants to see every minute misused; it is for us to make every minute count for God.

"How? Not by a frenzied rushing to pack a quart of activity into a pint pot of time (a common present-day error), but by an ordered life-style in which, within the set rhythm of toil and rest, work and worship, due time is allotted to sleep, family, wage-earning, homemaking, prayer, recreation, and so on, so that we master time instead of being mastered by it."[4]

Others Will Take Notice

God designed the Sabbath to be a sign of His touch of holiness upon our lives. Kay Arthur writes, "The words *sanctify*, *set apart*, *holy*, and *saint* come from the common root words *qadash* in the Hebrew and *hagios* in the Greek. For the first time in the Word of God, the purpose of and the command for the Sabbath is laid down before the children of Israel. The Sabbath is to be a sign between God and Israel throughout all their generations. The purpose of the Sabbath was 'that you may know that I am the Lord who sanctifies you' (Exodus 31:13) or 'that you may know that I am Jehovah-mekoddishkem.' As God made the Sabbath holy to the children of Israel, so He made the children of Israel holy, or set them apart, unto Himself."[5]

We Christians are God's chosen people, set apart to take hold of His power on this earthly plane and live holy lives. The idea of the Sabbath was a unique one when God commanded it. The gods of the nations around the Israelites did not practice it. In fact, back then as it is now, busyness and performance were hailed as signs of progress and innovation. After week upon week of observing Christians enjoy their Sabbath, complete with a "love feast" (the communal meal of worship), the Romans accused them of holding obscene orgies. They thought those Christians were enjoying the Sabbath too much! My question is, What's happened since?

The Harrison family probably made a lasting impression when they traveled across the country in horse-drawn wagons during California's gold rush. As devout Methodists, they refused to travel on Sundays and instead spent the time resting, worshiping, and reading their Bibles. As they did, other travelers passed and taunted them, saying there wouldn't be any gold left in California when they arrived. But in the end, God showed Himself faithful as the Harrisons not only caught up with the ones who had passed them but arrived first at the gold fields. Their own health and the health of their animals was better than that of those who hadn't taken the time to rest.[6]

Isn't the Lord wonderful? He gives us a gift of rest and remembrance for our benefit and then uses that gift to help others see how great He is. Taking a Sabbath rest will restore us so that our joy will be apparent and others will notice! That's a win-win-win situation—for God, for us, and for unbelievers!

Sunday Driving with God

Not only is the Sabbath rest a testimony to others, it's a step of growth in our walk with God. Irene shared with me how her faith grew as she kept the Fourth Commandment. As a child, she had always liked school and tried to stay near the top of the class with her best friend. This often meant staying up late, even after the other children in her neighborhood had gone to bed. If she hadn't finished her homework by Sunday afternoon, she would take that time to do it, but as a result, Irene began to dread the weekends because she never found time to rest.

One day, while feeling exhausted, the Lord gently whispered in her heart, "You don't have to do homework on Sundays."

"The voice was so caring," she told me. "I didn't hesitate to obey. I began to look forward to my day of rest. Yet my grades never suffered and I looked forward to every weekend's rest from my home*work*!"

Irene also shared with me the interesting fact that mules that work down in mines have to be brought up to the light every seven days or they go blind. You and I can go spiritually blind if we don't take time for Sabbath rest. But if we do take advantage of this gift from God, our faith will grow because we'll see that God can use the other six days to complete everything He plans to do through us.

Pride Goeth before the Fall (into Bed)

Another benefit of keeping the Sabbath is the reduction of our pride. Dorothy wrote, "To act as if the world cannot get along without our work for one day in seven is a startling display of pride that denies the sufficiency of our generous Maker."

Pride says, "I'm so important that I must continue my duties each and every day forever." Humility counters it by understanding that none of us is necessary, but God uses us regardless. If we obey Him by keeping a Sabbath rest, He can provide the time and energy to complete what He intends to accomplish.

I've seen that over and over again as I've faced writing deadlines and felt I couldn't possibly complete them without working on Sunday. But as I obeyed and kept the Sabbath "set apart," somehow, I don't know how, God caused those projects to be completed on time.

Are you falling into bed late on Sunday night having worked all day instead of resting? Put your pride to the side and try following God's commandment. With a day of rest you may be surprised at all you get done. I certainly have been.

A Taste of Heavenly Rest

The Sabbath is a preview of our future blessings in heaven. When we enjoy the constant personal presence and love of our Savior and God in heaven, there won't be any effort expended. If for one day a week we can attain to a little bit of that sense of heaven down here on earth, we will be more likely to enjoy the rest of the week.

Just think how different heaven will be from earth! Here we strive for approval by being as productive as we can. In heaven, there won't be a shred of doubt about God's total love. Here our bodies experience the wear and tear of working day in and day out. In heaven there are no such things as wear and tear. Well-known Christian author Patsy Clairmont says it this way: "This body is just a temporary time suit. (Can't you hear it ticking?) It's the only one we get before heaven's new, improved version, which will be complete with eternal vision."[7]

Your "Being" And Your "Doing"

Although people tend to measure success through accomplishments, God measures success with the growth of our character. The Sabbath commandment reminds us that as we obey Him, we are demonstrating the quality of our character rather than our ability to get a job done.

Alan Redpath writes, "If the child of God is always *in* for worship he gets spiritual indigestion. If he is always *out* in work he becomes spiritually ineffective, and we are all in danger of that."[8] The truly successful person is able to balance a growing spiritual life with an ability to work for God in His power.

That can be particularly difficult for the person serving God in full-time, vocational ministry. Moses happens to be the first full-time servant of God who is recorded as having an imbalance between his "doing" and his "being." As the Israelites traveled, Moses was the chief counselor for every problem the children of God faced. From sunup until sundown, a long line of people waited to bring their complaints and disagreements with their fellow Israelites before him for his decision. Moses was exhausted.

His father-in-law saw what was happening and told him:

What you are doing is not good. You and these people who come to you will only wear yourselves out. The work is too heavy for you; you cannot handle it alone. Listen now to me and I will give you some advice, and may God be with you. You must be the people's representative before God and bring their disputes to him. Teach them the decrees and laws, and show them the way to live and the duties they are to perform. But select capable men from all the people—men who fear God, trustworthy men who hate dishonest gain—and appoint them as officials over thousands, hundreds, fifties and tens. Have them serve as judges for the people at all times, but have them bring every difficult case to you; the simple cases they can decide themselves. That will make your load lighter, because they will share it with you. If you do this and God so commands, you will be able to stand the strain, and all these people will go home satisfied. (Exodus 18:17–23)

Moses was running himself ragged for no reason. By delegating some of his work to others he could free up his own time and others would also enjoy the benefits of ministering.

Those who are called into the ministry or who want to share the burdens of others often feel as though they must be available to solve every problem. If such a feeling is motivated by a need to be needed, then such people will burn out and fall short of experiencing the Sabbath rest that the writer of Hebrews talks about. "There remains, then, a Sabbath-rest for the people of God; for anyone who enters God's rest also rests from his own work, just as God did from his. Let us, therefore, make every effort to enter that rest, so that no one will fall by following [the Israelites'] example of disobedience" (Hebrews 4:9–11). The "Sabbath-rest" referred to here is a total trust in God that brings peace every moment, not just on a particular day.

Roger Barrier, a pastor, instituted wise rules that ensure his staff has an opportunity for a "Sabbath-rest."

We developed a plan limiting every minister at our church to a fifty-hour work week (including Sundays). The plan includes time compensation, because stress is cumulative. If some weeks require more than fifty hours, the ministers must balance with fewer hours over the next several weeks. In addition, our pastors must be home seven nights out of every fourteen. Each of us must take off a full twenty-four-hour day each week. It took several months, even years, for some of us to adjust. But we did it. Soon after implementing the plan, several of our ministers' wives quietly thanked me. They were seeing more of their husbands than they ever thought possible.

Having priorities that are based on "being" instead of "doing" helps us to take care of our spirits and bodies.

Lord, Teach Me to Celebrate

It is a good idea to ask God for His guidance in how to celebrate the Sabbath, because the answer is likely to vary from person to person.

Preparation is important, otherwise your Sabbath day will become just as stressful and harried as any other day. Known mainly for her novels, Robin Jones Gunn writes about that frustration in her poem "Holy Sabbath."

> This Lord's Day,
> I arose at six
> prayed
> showered
> nursed the baby
> fixed breakfast
> dressed
> ironed my husband's shirt
> bathed the baby

dressed the baby
found my husband's watch
curled my hair
changed the baby's diaper
answered the phone
put on some makeup
stuck a roast in the oven
packed the diaper bag
grabbed my Bible
dashed to the kitchen for Linda's casserole dish
ran to the car
and as I strapped my little angel
into his car seat
he vomited all over everything,
including me
and my only ironed dress.

Oh yes, Lord,
I shall remember this
Sabbath day.
However, I must confess,
I am completely stumped
on how to keep it holy.[9]

Most of us can relate. We may be able to avoid some of that stress by preparing on Saturday. Maybe we could lay out clothes, especially for the children, or plan our meals with ease of cooking in mind.

Myrtie told me, "On Saturday, I focus on praying for our pastor and the church family as a whole—to be what we should be to corporately worship well. My dad and my father-in-law were both pastors of churches so I am very aware of how heavy the Lord's Day workload can be, no matter how skillfully one's schedule is pre-planned."

On a different note, consider whether the recreation planned on Sunday is indeed "re-creation." So many of us use Sunday as a day for fun, and I believe that can be a part of God's plan: But if it's exhausting, then God's intention for that day has been lost. If our activities don't contribute to our focus on the Lord, then maybe those things should be considered for another day of leisure. Even though the commandment says not to work, it's also a commandment to focus on the Lord, to make the day "set apart" unto Him. It's a holy day, not a holiday.

As we seek to know how God wants us to keep the Sabbath holy, we should remember that God looks at our hearts. Edith Schaeffer writes, "There are no set rules which can be followed by each person because of our very diverse situations. Thank God that He 'looks upon the hearts.' He knows who truly loves Him; He knows who has a desire both to be and do that which would be pleasing to Him."[10]

Here's a quote from Robin, who has a refreshing perspective. "Keeping the Sabbath means taking time away from the everyday. You do something different than you normally do. You break out of the ruts and put on a fresh set of soul clothes."

What condition are your soul's clothes in? Tattered? Messy? Unkempt? How about "re-creating" them with a day of focusing on God?

Search Yourself

Does the Fourth Commandment seem legalistic or liberating to you?

⋙

How has neglecting the Sabbath affected you? How has observing it affected you?

⋙

Of all the reasons God gave us for observing a Sabbath, which is the most valuable to you and why?

⋙

In what ways do you take steps to "be" as well as "do"?

⋙

What are some ways you can prepare for the Sabbath? How is your way of observing the Sabbath unique to you?

The voice of parents

is the voice of gods,

for to their children

they are heaven's

lieutenants.

SHAKESPEARE

RULE V

You Are a Painting; Be Thankful for Your Artists

HONOR YOUR FATHER AND YOUR MOTHER,
SO THAT YOU MAY LIVE LONG IN THE LAND
THE LORD YOUR GOD IS GIVING YOU.

EXODUS 20:12

Once upon a time a family lived together and welcomed the mother's father into their home. He was helpful in the beginning and brought much joy to the mother, father, daughter, and son. When mom and dad needed to go out, he was always there to care for the children. When the plumbing stopped up, his experience came to the rescue.

In time, however, he became older and more feeble. He couldn't care for himself as well and instead of watching the children, they had to watch him. If a repair was needed, alas, he didn't even have the strength to pound a nail with a hammer. His wit was still a delight but taking care of him became a burden. After all, the children didn't need as much care now that they were older, and the parents didn't want to start caring for anyone again. So they put the old man in a nursing home and tried to find time to visit him.

One day, the mom happened to notice that her six-year-old son had a large piggybank. She hadn't realized he was saving his money. "Son, I'm so proud of you," she said. "You're really filling up your piggybank. Is it for anything special?"

"Yes," the son replied. "I'm saving so that I'll have the money when it's time to put *you* into a nursing home."

That little story is based on a Grimm fairy tale. Updated for today, it shows us the importance of the Fifth Commandment, which we now turn to. One of the main reasons God wants us to honor our parents is so that we will in turn be honored by our children.

Honor with a Purpose

I don't want to give the impression that we should never use nursing homes, convalescent homes, or board and care homes for the elderly. As we'll see, sometimes that's the most loving thing we can do. So what does it mean to follow this rule? To answer that question, we should probably start with a different one: What is honor?

The Hebrew word for *honor*, *kavod*, has a two-sided meaning. It means "to reverence" and "to be heavy." Together these meanings indicate that honoring means we "give weight" to someone as being valuable and important. It can also indicate that honoring can be a heavy responsibility—something not easily done.

Yet God did not say, "Honor your parents if they are good parents," or "Honor your parents if they treat you well as an adult." This rule is without qualification. Notice, however, that it is the only commandment with a promised reward for obedience. If we honor our parents, we will "live long," which is to say we will not only have longevity but enjoy it. God must have known we would need a little motivation to keep this one.

It is important to understand that this promise is like the promises of Proverbs. They aren't promises in the sense of being guarantees; they are statements about what generally happens. We can't claim that obeying this commandment will guarantee that we'll live to be a hundred. There are many people who honored their parents who died young and even before their parents. What God is saying is that overall life will be better for us if we honor our parents.

Honoring our parents is a *choice*. When we do not feel like honoring them or when we do not believe our parents deserve our honor, we would do well to assume the attitude of a United States Secret Service agent I talked to.

"It must be hard for you to protect someone whom you might not respect," I said. "After all, you are dedicated to give your life for such a person."

She replied, "We don't protect the *person*, we protect the *position*. Regardless of who is in the position, we are committed and trained to offer our lives for his or her safety."

That's the idea God wants us to have as we seek to honor our parents. We may not feel good about it. It may be a difficult choice, but like anything God asks us to do, He promises to provide the resources to do it if we ask Him.

Reach Out and Touch a Family Member

Joy Davidman wrote, "A society that destroys the family destroys itself."[1] As families disintegrate through divorce, same-sex marriages, and abuse, God's own image in the sight of children is being skewed for evil. David A. Seamands writes, "Mother and Dad are the skylight through which a child gets his or her first look at God."[2]

Our society's family unit has morphed from an extended family to a nuclear one. Within the extended family children grew up being influenced by many different kinds of people and relationships: parents, siblings, grandparents, aunts, uncles, and sometimes cousins. Contact with many different kinds of personalities and interaction between them helped children to learn how to deal with a variety of people and situations. Also, older people were regarded as valuable: sources of wisdom and instruction.

We will most likely never return to large extended families on a mass scale, but we can at least work to increase interaction between child and parent and grandparent. Keeping younger generations in contact with older ones will enable children to learn the history of their families, how the older generations dealt with life in the past, and how the historical events they study in school are regarded by those who lived through them.

Honoring our parents will bring about a respect for aged wisdom to counterbalance the all-too-popular, knee-jerk tendencies toward the new. Undue reverence for the new makes older people seem old-fashioned and out of step. But if we give true honor to our elders, we will consider their input valuable. Dr. Laura Schlessinger writes, "We must re-endow our elderly with the respect they deserve, to see them as national treasures rather than national relics."[3]

A final outcome of practicing honor in our families will be an appreciation for groups of people rather than the current tendency toward worshiping individuals. Our society today has a mentality of "one for one and all for one." Honor can help to restore the blessings of appreciating our family as a group or community. We will learn to appreciate family traditions that give us a sense of identity.

I appreciate my own family for all these reasons. I am in constant touch with my mother (my father is deceased) and my siblings and their families. We women of the family have been in a Bible study together for over ten years. We celebrate everyone's birthday with a family party. I try to spend time with my young nieces and nephews with the goal of being a rampart for them in the future when they go through the hard times of teenage mayhem. I've bowled in a league with my mother every Wednesday for over a dozen years.

We are blessed because our family is still living in the same area with only my sister living at a driving distance of four hours. Email and phone calls, along with frequent visits, keep us all connected with my sister. We make a concerted effort to remain in touch, and we enjoy a sense of tradition and connectedness as a result. Our mother is honored as an important member of our family, and we often reflect on the foundational values that our parents gave us.

Not every family can be as fortunate as ours, because people must move for various, legitimate reasons. But no matter where we are, we can still make efforts to honor our parents and other family members by staying in touch.

A Spiritual Dividend

Honoring our parents will help our spiritual growth. Now, this is something we may not welcome with delight right away, because our spiritual growth will usually occur only as we sacrifice ourselves. Earlier I mentioned our society's undue appreciation for individuals. What I didn't mention is that oftentimes such appreciation is for the individual looking back in the mirror! If we are always looking out for "number one," doing our very best to make life "pleasant" for ourselves, we will not want to take care of a needy parent in the home. We will not want to go visit a parent in a smelly nursing home, or transport a parent who can't drive to the grocery store.

Sacrificing for our parents doesn't come easy, but like sacrificing for a child, it will only be for a relatively short period of time.

I have heard from more than one friend about the joys of caring for a parent, even though there were inconveniences. My friend Neva took care of her mother and father for many years, which involved giving up the master bedroom for them. Neva always rejoiced in the time she could be with her parents, even though she had many other activities and ministries.

Neva is one of the most caring individuals I know. Did that caring quality come about because of the sacrifices or did she sacrifice because she is caring? It's difficult to say, but I know she has never felt a bit of regret, and God has honored her service.

Barbara Johnson writes, "Again and again I see folks who have had a lot of difficulties in life. . . . life puts you in the tumbler. You can come out crushed, or you can come out polished."[4]

Neva came out polished, and as long as we are following God's rules in His strength, we will too.

Receiving Grandma

Many young brides want to get going on the honeymoon after the ceremony and reception, but not Dee. She went to see her grandmother. Dee writes,

> At the time of my wedding my grandma's health was too poor for her to attend, so I promised I would visit her in my wedding dress at the nursing home after the wedding.
>
> As I walked toward my grandma with my wedding dress and veil on, her eyes were gleaming from underneath her bright, neon-pink baseball cap, which was given to her on Mother's Day. We hugged each other with tears of joy.
>
> I twirled around letting her see my dress with the long

train. Her eyes danced with pride and love as she fingered the pearled sequins. Grandma and I were floating on cloud nine as we made our way down the hallway. My new husband, Ted, joined our procession, pushing her wheelchair.

Everyone asked, "Who are you?"

I proudly held Grandma's hand. "I'm Rena Sanger's Granddaughter." Grandma beamed as they congratulated her.

I had transformed a nursing home into a reception hall without knowing it. I had only wanted to show Grandma my dress, but the overwhelmed residents stood in the hall cheering and laughing. Their faces wore looks of nostalgia: women sighing and reliving their own wedding days. The dingy hallway was filled with smiles and hands reaching out to feel the dress as they wanted to be part of the moment. Even the residents who usually sat with frowns were smiling and joining in.

Grandma felt like a queen that day. She was young again with no aches or pains to concern herself with. She laughed more than I had seen her laugh for many years.[5]

Later, Dee's grandmother passed away, yet Dee doesn't have any regrets. She doesn't wonder if she gave her grandmother the attention she deserved. "It can be hard to watch your loved ones grow old," says Dee. "But they too are on a journey and no matter what our age, we all have lessons to learn and to teach if we are willing."

Warning: Use Boundaries When Necessary

Honoring our parents does not mean we shut off our brains. Sometimes it becomes necessary to set up some boundaries. Hilary shared with me how she set boundaries up between her and her mother. She never felt like she had "cut the apron strings" from her mother, even after marrying her husband,

Cliff. She couldn't remember ever saying no to her mother's suggestions, forever fearing her mother's burning disapproval. If her mother suggested they go shopping, Hilary agreed even if she had planned to help Cliff work in the yard. If her mother suggested they have a family birthday party on a day that was inconvenient, Hilary would adjust her schedule. At times, Hilary felt like she hated her mother, and then hated herself for those ugly feelings.

But one day Hilary realized her mother really was making *suggestions*. She wondered whether she had been thinking her mother was trying to control her when that wasn't really the case. She prayed, asking the Lord to give her guidance and strength to respond when her mother made her next request.

It wasn't long before the next request came barreling at her.

"Honey, would you like to go to the theatre with me this Friday night?"

Hilary checked her schedule. She had something planned. She shot off a prayer for the right words, took a deep breath, and, "Mom, I'm sorry, but I already have something scheduled. I won't be able to go with you."

Silence followed.

And then, "Oh . . . Okay . . . Well, I guess I can ask Sandra to go instead."

Hilary and her mom talked a while longer and even though she sensed disappointment in her mom's voice, she was thrilled there hadn't been any anger. She did it!

Alicia wrote, "I love my parents dearly but have recently established some boundaries. It didn't go well at first. My father kept asking me if I was mad at him. After some trial and error I did find a successful strategy. Each time I saw them I made it a priority to hug them when I arrived and left. Also, when I spoke to them on the phone, I would tell them 'I love you.' My dad stopped asking me if I was angry with him."

Sometimes the boundaries will need to be more stringent. Stacey was sexually abused as a child but couldn't bring herself to do anything about it. The abuse lasted for three years, and her father's sin was never confronted. When Stacey married and had children, she felt uncomfortable when her children were in contact with her father, but she didn't want to keep them from him either. Through counseling she came to a fuller realization that she was putting her children in a dangerous situation, especially because her mother wanted them to spend nights and weekends at their house.

Stacey finally mustered the courage to confront her father and set some boundaries. It hasn't been easy, but she now has the peace of mind that comes with protecting her children.

Suzy struggled with the commandment to honor her parents because her mother refused to talk with her. She and her mother had a very difficult relationship all of Suzy's life. In counseling Suzy identified her mother as having multiple personalities, but Suzy chose to honor her mom. "I spent my whole life trying to please my mother," she said, "and yet she still disowned me. I prayed for God to help me forgive and honor her. I called her on holidays and sent presents. She never acknowledged them, but I did this out of obedience to God. Sometimes before calling her, I would get on my knees and say, 'This is for you, Lord. I will honor her and forgive her because You have done so much for me.'"

Anita found the appropriate boundary between her and her verbally abusive father. As an adult, she would become ill after visiting her father because he would call her names and tell her she could never do anything correctly. But she learned she could honor her dad regardless of his behavior:

I prayed for God to bless him despite his behavior toward me. Because we lived over five hundred miles away from him and my mother, I would call my mom frequently, speak with her, and send greetings on to my father. In this way I distanced myself from his verbal invectives.

I cannot make my father or anyone happy. Only God

can satisfy the human heart. My husband and I scheduled trips several times a year, stayed overnight in a nearby hotel, and limited the length of our visits. I found I could handle short episodes of abuse with my husband there afterwards for solace and strength. My dad died several years ago, yet I have great peace inside from honoring him, and I know he will be different in heaven.

Each situation and family is different and God will guide you whether your situation is like those just mentioned or completely different. Be assured that God loves you and doesn't want you to continue to suffer abuse. If you are still hurting from any kind of childhood trauma caused by your parents, it would be a good idea to seek professional Christian counseling because no two problems are identical and each calls for its own treatment.

As you look for help, remember Max Lucado's wise words: "God has proven himself as a faithful father. Now it falls to us to be trusting children. Let God give you what your family doesn't. Let him fill the void others have left. Rely upon him for your affirmation and encouragement."[6]

Becoming Honorable

The Fourth Commandment specifically addresses children, but parents should also take note. Are we being the kind of parents who deserve our children's honor? Are we developing godly qualities that will encourage our children to honor us?

I'll never forget the evening ritual that accompanied my daughter's bedtime. Darcy was a take-charge kind of person during the day and was not very open to hugs and attention. She was just too busy. But come bedtime, she softened. She would open up and talk. More importantly, she would listen to her mother. Unfortunately, I'm a morning person, and I couldn't wait to get her and her younger brother into bed so that I could go to bed myself. In time, however, I tried to save some energy because I realized bedtime was Darcy's daily appointment to receive my love. It is important for us to show our love to our children in ways they will recognize.

I recently watched an interview with Oscar de la Hoya, the accomplished boxer. Some of the interview focused on his relationship with his father. Oscar said he'd never heard his father give him praise or approval for his success as a boxer. His greatest dream, he said, was to get that approval.

My heart grieved for the young man. He was constantly striving for the love his father withheld. In the interview, Oscar said he wouldn't strive so intensely to succeed if he had received his father's love, and so he felt his father was doing him a favor. That was the reason for his success, he said.

But I don't buy it. Approval, love, and acceptance don't minimize desire for excellence; they feed it. And they do so in a much healthier way than emotional starvation does. Emotionally starving your child may motivate him or her, but it will leave an emptiness and in the end, bitterness.

If Oscar's dad is waiting for some "perfect" performance before giving his son the love, approval, and acceptance he craves, perhaps he should consider the reality that either his own or Oscar's life could end at any moment. We too should love our children freely, because we too have a limited amount of time to do so.

Another important part of being honorable parents is carrying out the discipline of our children. In love, we need to make our rules as well as the consequences for disobedience clear. In parenting seminars I give, I instruct parents to have a family meeting whereby parents must write down the rules of their household. Then, for each rule a corresponding consequence should be listed in case of disobedience. With a little encouragement children often point out the rules that are important to them, and they are also the most creative when it comes to thinking of consequences for each rule. Their input is to be taken seriously. The paper is then to be posted on the refrigerator for easy reference. If we quickly and calmly list our consequences for disobedience, instead of continually giving warnings, and then if we carry out those consequences when our children disobey, we will be one step closer to becoming parents our children will want to honor.

Ephesians 6:4 instructs, "Fathers, do not exasperate your children. . . ." Dr. Stuart Briscoe has a paraphrase for this: "Parents, don't drive your children nuts."[7] We drive our children nuts when we constantly nag and warn without following through with appropriate consequences.

We also need to give our children our time. I was recently in a meeting in which a pastor from another country was interviewed. He had just finished his summer-long sabbatical at our local seminary, and he and his family were returning home. He said, "I'm a very busy pastor in our home country and when we came, my children were looking forward to having more time with me. But I just couldn't resist being in the seminary library and all the fascinating classes I took. So now we're going back and we'll have more time there."

Yeah, right.

I felt deeply grieved at how blind this pastor was to the pattern he was starting. It's a good thing God commands this pastor's children to honor their father regardless of whether he deserves it. Otherwise, his children would have every right to say, "We don't have to honor you because you put your education before us."

Finally, honorable parents are parents who encourage and take interest in the goals and pursuits of their children. Samuel was one who didn't receive that as a child. Because Samuel's father was a superior athlete throughout his youth, he wanted Samuel to play football, baseball, and basketball in high school and college. He expected his son's success to surpass his own. When it didn't, Samuel's father was disappointed, and he said as much to Samuel. Even though Samuel did achieve a fair amount of success in basketball and track in high school, because he didn't want to take these sports any further, his father discounted what he did do.

Today, Samuel is a successful businessman because his father expected it of him, but Samuel's real passion is writing, teaching, and speaking. Samuel knows his father would be disappointed if he were to strike out into those areas, so he is working as a writer on the side and that gives him a greater sense of fulfillment.

"I love my parents," says Samuel, "and try to honor them with *who* I am through my godly character, not by *what* I do, whether business or writing. I will respect them even if they can't value who I am. So that I don't become discouraged by their philosophy, I try to remember God has wired me a certain way, and any attempts to rewire who I am will only result in blown fuses and short-circuits."

Samuel has begun to understand the truth of Max Lucado's words: "Having your family's approval is desirable but not necessary for happiness and not always possible. Jesus did not let the difficult dynamic of his family overshadow his call from God."[8]

Children are unique individuals. They have interests and passions that you may not have. But no matter how different your children are from you, they still need you to be interested in them. Your parental encouragement is priceless.

Forever Children

Jerry wrote this letter to his father on his father's eightieth birthday, only a few years before his father's death.

Dear Dad,
My earliest memories of you center mostly on your hands. Hands that were so much bigger and stronger than mine. Hands that were always so gentle, loving, and kind. Hands that I ould hold on to and were so dependable. I

remember going to the beach and holding on to your fingers with both of my hands and you dragging me through the water as I lifted up my feet. Hands that dried me off on the shore when I was shivering and cold. You showed me how to hold a pencil, form numbers, and write the alphabet as well as my name. I admired your penmanship and wished that some day I could write as well as you.

I saw your hands caress not only the children that God entrusted to you but also the woman you loved. I watched those hands of yours hold a sharp razor and run it across your face each morning. I vividly remember the days that I joined you when you drove a taxi. It was your hands on the wheel that guided us through traffic safely to the fare's destination. And many years later, it was those same strong hands that patiently and nervously taught me how to drive.

You were the one who came to my defense when I needed help, and you were the one who taught me many of the skills that I would need to successfully navigate my way through life. My continuing goal is to be just like the father and husband you have modeled for me; there is no course taught anywhere on how to be a man, but you have lived it in front of me all these years.

I love you,
Jerry[9]

What a beautiful tribute and loving way to honor a parent. I'm sure Jerry's father wasn't perfect, but Jerry focused on things he appreciated. Should we *never* look at the negative? That would be impossible and certain issues need to be addressed, but focusing on the positives will allow us to honor our parents in sincerity, as Jerry did.

Myrtie tells me, "My dad had very dogmatic opinions, but I always respected him. Even though my parents had serious flaws, I have always been thankful for the many job skills my dad taught me. Because of him, I am able to complete most tasks I begin. I see that as a positive influence in my life for which I honor my dad. I honor my mother for being in our home every day while I was growing up." Myrtie focuses on the positives, and as a result, she is at peace with the past.

But being at peace with the past will not happen completely until we forgive our parents for their inadequate parenting. We can't forget, but we can forgive. Forgiving our parents means no longer trying to hold them hostage with anger or bitterness. Nineteenth-century philosopher Edwin Hubbell Chapin said, "Never does the human soul appear so strong and noble as when it forgoes revenge and dares to forgive an injury."[10]

Robin wrote me saying, "As an adult, I have learned one way to honor my father and my mother is to stop blaming them for all of my faults, real and imagined. I finally came to the point where I said, 'I am what I am, good and bad, not only because of the way my parents raised me but because of the person I have decided to be.' To honor my father and my mother means I let them off the hook, I allow them to be human, I stop beating them up for their inadequacies, and I get on with being an adult myself."

We need somehow to realize that nothing happens without God's allowing it to happen—whether good, bad, or indifferent. Yes, even the horrible, cruel things. He allows the worst, and He intends to use it all for good. David Seamands wisely wrote, "God is not the Author of all events, but He is the Master of all events. This means that nothing has ever happened to you that God cannot and will not use for good if you will surrender it into His hands and allow Him to work."[11]

Romans 8:28 promises us, "And we know that in all things God works for the good of those who love him, who have been called according to his purpose." Forgiveness is made easier when we realize God was with us during our pain. He knew then, and He knows now, how He will use the pain for our benefit and His glory. Trust the Word of God; His promise is true.

How to Take Care of Aging Parents

The first letter of Timothy does not mince words about taking care of family: "If anyone does not provide for his relatives, and especially for his immediate family, he has denied the faith and is worse than an unbeliever" (1 Timothy 5:8).

With this in mind we should be comforted that God will guide each of us when our parents face old age. Love, as defined by evangelist Winkie Pratney, is choosing a person's highest good. When it comes to caring for our parents, love means doing whatever is best for *them*. If an elderly person is endangering people (including himself or herself) by driving, then we'll need to take away their driving privileges, even if they fight us. If a parent with Alzheimer's is physically abusive, then he or she may need to live in a board and care home with those trained to handle such situations.

Joan had taken care of her two beloved aunts until doing so had completely drained her and was taking a serious toll on her own family and work. It broke her heart to put her aunts into a rest home, but she could no longer provide the care they needed. When she expressed her sorrow to the nurses there, one replied, "Honey, we are on eight-hour shifts. You would be on twenty-four-hour shifts back to back."

Joan says, "Parents can be honored in many ways, but breaking down one's own health is not one of them."

When flight attendants give their pre-flight safety instructions, they always say the same thing about the oxygen masks. "If air pressure should drop within the cabin, oxygen masks will automatically drop from the ceiling. . . . For those of you with children, please put your own mask on first and then assist your children." The same principle applies to the care of our parents. If we're going to be of any help to them, we have to be in good shape ourselves.

The best way to take care of aging parents is to be honest about what's best for your parents and realistic about what's best for you.

Search Yourself

After reading about the Fifth Commandment,
what does "honor" mean to you?

⁂

What do you think is the most important reason
for honoring your parents?

⁂

Which blessing that comes from honoring your
parents is the most motivating to you?

⁂

What boundaries have you had to set in your
relationship with your parent(s)? Are there any
further boundaries you need to establish?

⁂

How would you like to grow as a parent so that
you will deserve the honor your children give you?

For thirty years I have tried to see the face of Christ in those with whom I differed.

BISHOP WHIPPLE

RULE
VI

Build Up, Don't Tear Down

YOU SHALL NOT MURDER.

EXODUS 20:13

I met her at our local park when both of us took our children there to play on the monkey bars. I knew she was a Christian and a pastor's wife for the local Methodist church. When we happened to be at the park at the same time we enjoyed visiting and sharing our thoughts about the Lord.

One day when we saw each other, she seemed a little sad. When I inquired, she replied, "Oh, I had a miscarriage last week."

I hadn't even known she was pregnant. Having not experienced a miscarriage myself, it didn't really seem like a big deal. No one I knew had gone through this either, so I felt inadequate to respond to her. In my confusion, I blurted out, "Oh, well, you can have another child."

Her face fell a little more, but not knowing what to do, I ignored it and continued talking about anything I could to divert us from the awkwardness.

Only after I got home and began thinking about what a miscarriage really is did I realize how insensitive I had been. She had experienced a death, and I had added to her grief by minimizing her loss.

So what does my story have to do with a chapter on murder? After all, I didn't pull out a gun and shoot her, right?

But I had, in a sense. I pulled out the gun of insensitive words and killed a bit of her spirit. From the "murder" God talks about in Exodus coupled with some of Jesus' comments, we will see that a biblical perspective of murder includes more than ending a life. Mean words, physical assaults, hatred, even prejudice—all can rightly be placed under the sin of murder.

A Christian Interpretation

In the original Hebrew, inscribed on stone by God Himself, the Sixth Commandment consisted of only two words: *Lo tirtza-akh. Lo* means *No.* And according to *The Hebrew and English Lexicon of the Old Testament* by Brown, Driver, and Briggs, the second word has as its root in the word *rahtz-akh,* which can be translated with three different meanings:

- Don't kill the body of yourself or someone else.
- Don't break, bruise, or crush (referring to someone's spirit).
- Don't batter or shatter, either physically, verbally, or through humiliation.[1]

Also, the word *rahtz-akh* implies the violent killing of a personal enemy or through "wrongful death." Because of the word used here, and in comparison with other scripture, we discover that not all killing is the same in God's eyes. Exodus

21:12–14 reads: "Anyone who strikes a man and kills him shall surely be put to death. However, if he does not do it intentionally, but God lets it happen, he is to flee to a place I will designate. But if a man schemes and kills another man deliberately, take him away from my altar and put him to death." The "place" for the more fortunate of the above two "killers" is called "a city of refuge," where he would be safe until the death of the High Priest. Then he was absolved of responsibility.

But isn't all this rather unneeded? Why did God have to give such a commandment in the first place? It's so obvious we shouldn't take people's lives. Didn't the Hebrews know that?

At the time God gave the Ten Commandments people killed indiscriminately. People killed for no reason at all and suffered no consequences. Life was cheap. In addition, the former rules of other nations that had been established were not fair. For instance, one of the laws of the Hammurabi's code from Babylon said, "If a man strikes a gentleman's daughter that she dies, his own daughter is to be put to death; if a poor man's, the slayer pays one half mina." Joy Davidman writes, "For Hammurabi and his times, the individual and individual guilt were nothing, the loss in value to the clan or family the sole consideration."[2]

God steps in and establishes something totally new: fairness and an emphasis on the value of the individual. God says, "I made people in my image and anyone who destroys a life is destroying my creation."

Dr. Stuart Briscoe writes, "If God makes man for eternity and gives him the ability to function in relationship to Him, anyone who kills that man destroys what God had in mind. The destroyer shakes his fist in the face of God."[3]

Although every Christian must make up his or her own mind, I believe the rules God gives regarding murder in Moses' writings refer to the legitimacy of capital punishment. Not all Christians agree on that, but God seems to me to be saying, "Don't take anyone's life and if you do, your own life will be ended by my agents of righteousness." God told Noah, "And for your lifeblood I will surely demand an accounting. I will demand an accounting from every animal. And from each man, too, I will demand an accounting for the life of his fellow man. Whoever sheds the blood of man, by man shall his blood be shed; for in the image of God has God made man" (Genesis 9:5–6). With the establishment of the Ten Commandments, God put an exclamation point on that principle.

But the majority of us don't want to kill anybody, and neither will most of us have the awful burden of deciding whether to enact capital punishment (God be with those who do). So, do we need to pay attention to the Sixth Commandment? Is it relevant to us?

Jesus and Murder

Jesus picked up the Sixth Commandment, blew the dust off of it, and said, "Hey, this is for you too." Well, that's a paraphrase. What he actually said was:

> You have heard that it was said to the people long ago, "Do not murder, and anyone who murders will be subject to judgment." But I tell you that anyone who is angry with his brother will be subject to judgment. Again, anyone who says to his brother, "Raca," is answerable to the Sanhedrin. But anyone who says, "You fool!" will be in danger of the fire of hell.
>
> Therefore, if you are offering your gift at the altar and there remember that your brother has something against you, leave your gift there in front of the altar. First go and be reconciled to your brother; then come and offer your gift.
>
> Settle matters quickly with your adversary who is taking you to court. Do it while you are still with him on the way, or he may hand you over to the judge, and the judge may hand you over to the officer, and you may be thrown into prison. I tell you the truth, you will not get out until you have paid the last penny. (Matthew 5:21–26)

Our Savior says, "Hate is like murder, and so is resentment." Now that's stepping on our toes a bit! After all, some people really tick us off! Some people have really hurt us! I don't want to murder them (although, truth be told, sometimes that seems like a good idea too), I just want to injure them through my pouting, moping, bitterness, and resentment. I'll show them!

Those were my attitudes during the time that anger ruled my life over twenty-two years ago. At that time, Larry and I had been married seven years and we had two children, two-year-old Darcy and newborn Mark. I felt abandoned by Larry because he worked two jobs and had a flying hobby. He was never home. I *was* home, with a toddler who didn't want to cooperate with my toilet training program and an infant who kept me awake at night nursing. It seemed that Larry was completely insensitive to my needs, and I had expected when we married that he would always be my Prince Charming, responsible for my happiness.

The angrier I got at Larry, the more I mistreated Darcy. In time, my reactions toward her became so intense and damaging that I had to admit I was abusing my precious daughter. I also had murderous thoughts toward my husband, Larry, because I blamed him for my inability to live a godly life. After all, if he were meeting my needs, I would be joyful and content.

I remember when one day, after Larry announced he would be off flying for the day, I was furious because it seemed like he was always gone. I threw an apple at him as he left the house. The apple smashed against the door that he had just closed behind him. Then in my fury, I stamped into my bedroom and knelt by my bed. I clasped my hands together and spit out, "God! Make his plane crash!"

Another time when he made me angry, I prayed, "Lord! Cause him to have an accident so that he'll be a paraplegic. That way he'll stay home!"

As I reflect on that time of great anger and hate, I'm ashamed to think of all that I did. But as I've shared my story with others, both in print and through my speaking, I've seen God use my experience for His glory. Others have been helped.

They are encouraged because I can also share that God healed our family. Although that doesn't always happen with every hurting family, we were able to take hold of God's power and help and become the loving family God wanted us to be. God first strengthened me to become the patient mother He wanted me to be by showing me the underlying causes of my anger. Then through a marriage retreat, God began the healing process that Larry and I needed to become the best friends and lovers that we are today.

Our daughter, Darcy, is now twenty-four, and she and I have a wonderful relationship and have written a book together called *Staying Friends with Your Kids*. Larry and I coauthored *When the Honeymoon's Over*, and recently we celebrated twenty-nine years of marriage. It's amazing to think God can even use murderous thoughts and intentions for good, but He can.

During that time of such out-of-control anger, I didn't understand my hatred rivaled the murder forbidden in the Ten Commandments. In contrast, let's look at some things Jesus did:

- Jesus rebuked His disciples for wanting to call down fire from heaven to get rid of their enemies (Luke 9:54–55).
- Jesus healed the High Priest's servant's ear that Peter impulsively cut off at Jesus' arrest (Matthew 26:52–53).
- Jesus refused a fight for His release during his trial (John 18:36).
- Jesus allowed His enemies to spit in His face (Matthew 26:67).

Philippians 2:5–8 says we are supposed to emulate Christ in our attitude: "Your attitude should be the same as that of Christ Jesus: Who, being in very nature God, did not consider equality with God something to be grasped, but made himself nothing, taking the very nature of a servant, being made in human like-ness. And being found in appearance as a man, he humbled him-self and became obedient to death—even death on a cross!"

Jesus loved everyone so much that He wasn't merely *with-out* hate, He was *with* a very active love. The apostle John commanded us, "Dear children, let us not love with words or tongue but with actions and in truth" (I John 3:18). I'll bet John had his good friend Jesus in mind when he said that.

The Motivations of Obvious Murder

When we think of murder, we often think of the more obvious examples that currently plague our nation: killings, abortion, euthanasia, and suicide. Such traumatic and damaging events can be motivated by anger or fear or both. In each, lives are impacted forever. No wonder our loving Lord wanted us to avoid such hurtful actions.

The killing at Columbine High School in Littleton, Colo-rado, seems to have been motivated by anger. The two young men who killed twelve people evidently believed their class-mates didn't care about them. They wanted revenge regard-less of whether their perceptions were correct or not. We'll never know all of their motivations, but God is using even that horrible event for good.

Darrell Scott, father of two of the victims (one of whom was killed) addressed the Subcommittee on Crime for the House Judiciary Committee of the United States House of Rep-resentatives on Thursday, May 27, 1999. Here's an excerpt from what he said:

> The real villain lies within our own hearts. Political pos-turing and restrictive legislation is not the answer. The young people of our nation hold the key. There is a spiri-tual awakening taking place that will not be squelched! . . . We do need a change of heart and an humble acknowledg-

ment that this nation was founded on the principle of simple trust in God.

As my son Craig lay under that table in the school library and saw his two friends murdered before his very eyes, he did not hesitate to pray in school. I defy any law or politician to deny him that right!

I challenge every young person in America and around the world to realize that on April 20, 1999, at Columbine High School—prayer was brought back to our schools. Do not let the many prayers offered by those students be in vain. . . . My daughter's death will not be in vain. The young people of this country will not allow that to happen.[4]

Darrell Scott's courageous stand is one of many prompted by the Littleton shooting. God is using this tragedy as a wake-up call for our country, even as He grieves with the hurting families who lost loved ones. Romans 8:28 tells us God will use *everything* for good.

"Abortion stops a beating heart" reads a well-known bumper sticker. Yes, it does, but what is it that drives people to abortion? Most of us immediately think of the more selfish of motivations like not wanting the financial inconvenience of a child, but Frederica Mathewes-Green, author of *Real Choices: Offering Practical, Life-Affirming Alternatives to Abortion* (Questar, 1994), found that the real motivation is usually much different. She is currently director of communications for the National Women's Coalition for Life and directed the Real Choices research project in which she interviewed many women in different cities across the United States who had had abortions. She writes, ". . . as I listened to these women, and others in cities all across America, a surprising theme emerged. In nearly every case, the abortion was undertaken to fulfill a felt obligation to another person: a parent (and then, most often, her mother) or the father of her unborn child. The predictable barriers of housing, jobs, and money faded rapidly in significance when these women were faced with a loved one's disapproving frown. They needed personal support and encouragement more than any material aid."[5]

We Christians must be the first to help alleviate the fears of those who are considering abortion. It's easy to say, "Don't do it," but fear is a strong motivation. God may call you and I to offer assistance by taking in an unmarried, pregnant woman or by volunteering at a crisis center. We can all take part in a march for life or stand outside an abortion clinic for a few moments of prayer. At the very least, when we drive by an abortion clinic we can pray for the people who work there and for the people who go there for answers to difficult problems. We can pray against evil. As we do, we'll be encouraging others to obey God's sixth rule.

A type of murder that more and more of us will face in the future is euthanasia. When a loved one dies slowly, it's difficult to resist the temptation to speed death along, thinking that by doing so we will be reducing pain and anguish. I'm not talking about taking away extra measures to prolong life; I'm talking about giving someone a death-effecting pill.

Make no mistake. Only God has the right to decide when to end someone's life. "The Lord brings death and makes alive; he brings down to the grave and raises up" (1 Samuel 2:6).

Author Gary L. Thomas identifies that the practice of euthanasia is based in fear. "Advocates of physician-assisted suicide have tapped into the frightened psyche of our aging and ailing population, addressing a fear that, unfortunately, politicians, physicians, and the church are refusing to address."

Thomas interviewed Edmund Pellegrino, whose medical practice is dedicated to helping those who want to end their lives because of illness by addressing their needs in literally life-giving ways.

Thomas writes, "In Pellegrino's experience, the demand for PAS [physician-assisted suicide] is a shortcut that attempts to address legitimate concerns in illegitimate ways. That is why he believes it is important to maintain the distinction between active and passive euthanasia, or, as he prefers to call it, between killing and letting die."

About one of Pellegrino's patients Thomas writes, "Once these needs were met, the patient thanked Pellegrino for not responding to his earlier request to die. 'The most valuable days of my life have been the last days I have spent,' he said."[6]

I saw the truth of this patient's claim in the life of my mother's second husband, Bud. Bud died slowly from prostate cancer while my mother took care of him with the help of hospice care in their home. Fortunately, few drugs were needed to spare him pain. Over the months when he lay immobile, he understood that he needed Jesus to cleanse him of his sins.

One day, after his nephew had spoken to him about Jesus' death on the cross, he told me, "I'm trying to trust God for salvation."

I replied, "Bud, you don't have to *try*. You can ask Jesus into your heart and know you are saved right now."

"Really?" he said.

A moment later, he repeated a prayer asking Jesus to forgive him and enter his heart as his Lord and Savior. After that precious moment we opened our eyes, and Bud wiped away tears. Over the following months as he slowly died, he expressed his gratitude to the Lord for the time he had left to learn more about his new faith. If we had somehow hurried his death, in fear that he might suffer, he would not have had the joy of knowing he would be joining Jesus when he died.

Even though fear is what most often motivates euthanasia, usually both anger and fear are involved in what we call "suicide." When people commit suicide, they have fallen for the lie that God is insufficient, and we all know who the father of lies is.

Just yesterday, I met Donna at one of my speaking engagements. She told me how four years before she had stood outside the welfare office trying to find the courage to jump in front of a bus so that she could end her life. She had been on drugs, was on welfare, and had no hope for her life. As she stood there, she kept thinking, "My son will be better off without me. I've got to do it."

A bus went by with so much speed, the wind forced her back a step. She wondered if God had meant that bus for her. Within a short time a minister came by and, led by the Lord, spoke words of life-changing help to Donna. She was directed to a nearby church, which helped her turn her life around. Now she is off drugs and welfare, working, and used by God to write poetry for people she meets. Her poetry is inspired by God to such an extent that without knowing a person, she can write words that truly minister to him or her.

She told me as she looked adoringly at her seven-year-old son, "If I'd taken my life, my son would have been devastated, and I wouldn't have the joy of seeing him grow up. I had fallen for Satan's lie that I was hopeless. But now I know that with God, there is always hope."

Satan uses killings, abortion, euthanasia, and suicide to ruin the world that God created so beautifully. But these aren't the only devices of our enemy. The ones I'll mention next are probably more widely applicable.

Crushing a Spirit

Killings, abortion, euthanasia, and suicide are the manifestations of murder most obviously related to the Sixth Commandment. If we can agree, however, that the Hebrew definition for the word "murder" refers equally to the crushing of another person's spirit, then we are no doubt faced with other, subtler types of murder.

Although it may not affect other people unless they notice, "road rage" is a kind of murder. I'm not talking about pulling out a gun and shooting someone through a car window, though if we were really honest, we would admit our temptations to do so. No, I'm talking about reviling someone who has inadvertently or even intentionally inconvenienced us with their driving. Road rage is when another person's driving makes us "nuts!" Robin confesses to this "murder." She says:

> If there was a body count of all the people I've murdered while in my car, we would have no overpopulation problems. My most nasty, hurtful, thoughtless, and godless tirades of name-calling are directed at my fellow drivers on the road. It wasn't until I was reading and studying Proverbs that I was convicted by the potential damage I could be doing. Proverbs 31:26 says, "She speaks with wisdom, and faithful instruction is on her tongue." Meditating on that challenging character quality rehabilitated my words and attitudes.
>
> One day I was glad I had changed my ways. I was waiting at a drive-through window for my order of milk shakes. While they made the shakes, the attendant handed me and my companion our straws, and I hit mine against the steering wheel to get the paper off. About that time, a car pulled up behind us and honked. With my newfound serenity behind the wheel, I refrained from jerking my head around to scowl at the impatient driver. After a few minutes, I calmly said to my friend, "I can't imagine why that turkey would honk at me like that."
>
> She laughed out loud and said, "Robin, that was you, goofy! You honked your own horn when you hit the steering wheel with your straw!"
>
> Thank goodness I had only made a mild idiot of myself and we could have a good laugh! Now I know that it doesn't matter if the person I am "murdering" is encased in steel and will never see me again. That person is a child of God, someone for whom Christ died. Besides, all that adrenaline collects in my own body, not theirs.

How true! The anger from road rage doesn't hurt the other driver at all. It only hurts us.

Another instance of "murder" happens when we try to change someone into whom we think they should be. Whenever someone tells us we should think the way they do, or act the way they do, we are hurt because we are not being accepted and loved for who we are. Dianne went through this as a child when her parents punished her severely for expressing any unpleasant emotions. Her parents most likely thought they were teaching her well, but in fact, they were crushing her spirit with conditional love, causing her to bury her anger until it surfaced inappropriately.

She says, "For a long time I denied ever being angry, but now I know that has not been the case. I am learning to set boundaries and communicate more with others about how I feel and what I expect."

Alicia shared with me another example of subtle "murder." She wrote me to say,

> As a competitive tennis player, my overzealous, dog-eat-dog attitude was concerning me because I was not showing love for my fellow man. I prayed about it for weeks and as I was playing one day, with hate in my heart for my opponent, God answered my prayers. I was on the court during a point and felt this overwhelming joy and peace. My whole attitude changed in an instant. Instead of wishing my opponent would make a mistake, I focused on *my* game. Instead of shunning her when we walked past one another to switch sides, I found myself telling her how nicely she played and building her up. I started seeing tennis in a whole different light. Instead of going out there to win, I was going out there to show the love of Jesus Christ. And you know what? I haven't lost since, because to "lose" in any real sense is to be hateful.

In marriage, hopefully we won't have a competitive spirit (although that can happen also), but we can easily slip into "murderous" attitudes when we crush the spirit of our mate by not listening. A husband can crush a wife's spirit if he quickly and insensitively offers a solution to a problem his wife is trying to express. Most women are not interested in quick-fix solutions to complex problems. They want to be heard, to be understood.

On the other hand, a wife can be guilty of crushing her husband's spirit when she uses cruel words or interrupts him.

Both husband and wife need to prevent crushing each other's spirit by learning how the other wants or needs to be loved. Each of us has a different definition of love, and we may be trying to make our spouse feel loved by doing what's important to us instead of what is important to him or her. When Larry and I share this concept at marriage retreats, we give every husband and wife an opportunity to share with each other how they most like to be shown love. People are often amazed at what their spouses tell them.

Another example of "murder" is prejudice. It must grieve our Lord deeply to see the hatred of prejudice rooted even in the hearts of His own people. Many years ago, I saw its ugliness in a fellow Christian. As a new Christian, I enjoyed talking with those who knew the Lord where I worked. One day, the issue of prejudice against black people came up, and my Christian friend said, "But don't you know that they are the descendants of Cain, and we're not supposed to have anything to do with them?"

I was speechless. I didn't know how to counter such thinking. This woman attended a conservative Southern California church and had seemed to be a loving Christian member of the Body of Christ. She needed to hear the perspective of June Cerza Kolf. She writes:

When my friend, Sadie, was taken to the emergency room at a local hospital, I rushed over to be with her as soon as I received the news.

Sadie was both surprised and pleased to see me. "How did you get them to let you in?" she asked, knowing visitors were not usually allowed in the emergency room.

I, too, had been concerned about that on the drive over. However, I knew Sadie needed a friend to comfort her. In desperation, I had decided if worse came to worst, I would be forced to tell a lie and say I was Sadie's sister. I hoped I wouldn't have to resort to that and I asked the Lord for guidance.

After I explained all this to Sadie, she threw back her head in hearty laughter. While I was trying to figure out why Sadie was laughing, I glanced down at our clasped hands—my very white one held gently between her two black ones.[7]

We all need that "color-blind" attitude to overcome the murderous attitude of prejudice. Regardless of whether we were born into a family of prejudiced thinking and were influenced from an early age, or whether a member of another race has traumatized us in some way, we each must allow God's love for every single person to permeate our hearts. Jesus had every person in mind when he hung on the cross.

The quote by Bishop Whipple that opened this chapter can be our watchword. If we can see the face of Jesus superimposed over every face we encounter, regardless of color or nationality, we'll take the first step in softening our hardened hearts.

As we face whatever murderous thoughts and feelings we each experience, God can help us become more compassionate and understanding of those who are misunderstood in society.

The Purpose of Temptation

Before the very first murder occurred, God warned the eventual perpetrator to guard his heart.

In the course of time Cain brought some of the fruits of the soil as an offering to the Lord. But Abel brought fat portions from some of the firstborn of his flock. The Lord looked with favor on Abel and his offering, but on Cain and his offering he did not look with favor. So Cain was very angry, and his face was downcast. Then the Lord said to Cain, "Why are you angry? Why is your face downcast? If you do what is right, will you not be accepted? But if you do not do what is right, sin is crouching at your door; it desires to have you, but you must master it. (Genesis 4:3-7)

God warned Cain ahead of time that sin wanted to destroy him, but Cain fell into temptation, killed his brother, and then he had to leave his parents and strike out on his own. We certainly don't want something like that to happen to us, so how do we go about resisting temptation?

We can start by understanding why God allows temptation and then take a look at the specific temptations of our own lives. The reason God allows temptation is because by temptation we are driven to depend on God. If we were never tempted toward evil, we would not need to focus on God or grow in our ability to seek Him. "No temptation has seized you except what is common to man. And God is faithful; he will not let you be tempted beyond what you can bear. But when you are tempted, he will also provide a way out so that you can stand up under it" (1 Corinthians 10:13). We will not see that provision of "a way out" unless we are turning to God for His help.

Famous Dutch religious writer Thomas à Kempis wrote, "Many people try to run away from temptations only to fall even harder. Trying to escape is not the solution. What makes us stronger than any of our enemies is patience and humility. If you only try to avoid temptations outwardly (rather than pluck them out by the roots) you will not get very far. Like weeds in a poorly cultivated garden, they will soon return worse than before."[8]

We need to learn to appreciate temptation's capacity for refining us.

Anger, Fear, and the Importance of Yielding

As you and I evaluate the underlying causes of our anger, we will have greater strength to be the loving Christians God wants us to be. Ephesians 4:26 says, "In your anger do not sin." It doesn't say not to get angry. God the Father shows his wrath and Jesus the Son became angry, yet neither has ever sinned. Anger is not sin in itself, but if we angrily respond in disobedience to God, that *is* sin.

We often become angry because we feel like we won't be heard correctly. Sometimes we are afraid of listening to other people's points of view because they may be right! Billy Graham wrote, "It is fear that makes us unwilling to listen to another's point of view, fear that our own ideas may be attacked. Jesus had no such fear . . . and we would do well to learn from Him."[9]

Jesus didn't have any fear because he had complete faith and trust that his Father was in charge of everything that was happening to and around him. He didn't have a need to convince anyone of anything, only to represent his Father truthfully. He definitely spoke the truth, and sometimes even in anger, but his motives were always righteous.

We can have the same peace knowing God is in charge. We only need to be concerned about what God thinks of us, not others.

Martin Luther wrote,

When two goats meet on a narrow bridge over deep water, what do they do? The bridge is so narrow they can neither turn around nor pass each other. If they fight they may fall into the water and be drowned.

They resolve the problem quite naturally. One lies down and the other passes over. Neither is injured.

People can learn a similar tactic. It is better to yield a little than to fall into raucous discord with others.[10]

Yielding reveals our trust in God's promise to meet our true needs with His abundant riches (cf. Philippians 4:19). Alan Redpath wrote, "The greatest thing we can ever be in our lives is a stepping-stone to Jesus, and stepping-stones are designed to be walked on, and that hurts, especially if those who walk on us are our friends."[11]

Italian priest Lawrence Scupoli goes even further than Redpath and says, "Our problem is conforming with the will of God. We don't know how to yield to him. We are reluctant to submit to his judgments. We are not able to imitate Christ humbled and crucified. We have not found a way to love our enemies, or to see them as instruments used by God to train us in self-denial."[12]

Scupoli points to the importance of recognizing trials as instruments to prune away our godlessness. When we're under the stress of a crisis or a conflict with someone, we will have to make a choice whether to respond with love and patience or with anger. At that moment, God is asking, "Will you love this person and give up your murderous responses? Will you trust Me to be in control rather than trying to make sure things happen the way *you* want?"

The Way of Love

Jesus said that to show we love him, we must keep his commandments and love others. All the commandments are wrapped up in the bow of love. If we love, we will automatically keep the commandments. But how do we love specifically in regard to the Sixth Commandment?

The most difficult part is forgiving. Forgiveness is a choice, and its opposite, revenge, is also a choice. Paul wrote to the Roman church, "Do not repay anyone evil for evil. Be careful to do what is right in the eyes of everybody. If it is possible, as far as it depends on you, live at peace with everyone. Do not take revenge, my friends, but leave room for God's wrath, for it is written: 'It is mine to avenge; I will repay,' says the Lord. On the contrary: 'If your enemy is hungry, feed him; if he is thirsty, give him something to drink. In doing this, you will heap burning coals on his head.' Do not be overcome by evil, but overcome evil with good" (Romans 12:17–21).

God has everything in His hands, and He will do the right thing.

Dianne told me, "I try very hard not to hold grudges, because over the years I have observed that doing so only hurts the one holding the grudge! I ask God to take the hurt and help me to forgive. It's not easy and doesn't always happen overnight. Some things take time, but if I'm sincere, God always answers my prayer and helps me."

Jeanne shared with me that she was upset with Patty, a woman whom she had allowed to stay in her home. Patty was out of a job, and Jeanne wanted to help this new Christian get back on her feet. But having Patty live with her was frustrating because Patty never picked up after herself and Jeanne was used to a neat and tidy apartment.

When Patty suddenly moved out, Jeanne became more angry because Patty never admitted to her sloppiness and furthermore, she never thanked Jeanne for helping her.

Jeanne and Patty lost track of each other. Years later, Jeanne says, "I realized how this grudge was imprisoning my spiritual life. The parable of the unmerciful servant in Matthew 18 became my personal story. I knew what I had to do. First, I had to confess my grudge as sin. Then I had to see why God had allowed Patty to come into my life. Finally, I needed to take the initiative in making amends."

That's exactly what Jeanne did. She was able to find Patty's current address, and she sent a letter confessing her sin. Although it was very difficult, it freed Jeanne of the bitterness that was poisoning her own life.

A while later Jeanne was surprised to receive a reply from Patty, admitting her own part in the problem and forgiving Jeanne for hers.

Christina tells about the time she and her husband temporarily took in her elderly and severely ill great-aunt. After the aunt had lived with Christina for a couple of months, the aunt's brother, with whom she had been living previously, came and asked his sister to do something that would have been profitable to him but devastating to her, emotionally and physically.

Christina says,

> As I firmly took my aunt aside, her brother stomped out of the house. I was so angry I was shaking. I remember the Lord bringing to mind "Bless; do not curse." I stood there in my kitchen blessing my uncle in the name of the Father, and of the Son, and of the Holy Spirit. I repeated this until my heart came in line with the words, and I stopped shaking. My aunt calmed down as well.
>
> God has taught me to bless those who hurt me and in this way to place coals of fire on their heads. This used to sound like revenge to me ("I'll bless them Lord, so you can get them.") until I researched scripture. In biblical times, early in the morning a person from each household would head for the common fire in the center of town and place burning coals in a basket and then carry them home on top of his or her head. This would provide warmth, light, and fuel to cook their meals. We can do that physically through providing for the needs of those who hurt us, spiritually by interceding in prayer for them, and emotionally by sending them a card or speaking in love. In the mere act of saying, "Lord forgive me for being angry, please bless that person . . . please supply their need," I am freed from my murderous thoughts.

It's not easy to bless instead of curse, but it is the path of forgiveness and the key for releasing our murderous intentions.

Search Yourself

What is murder?

How does Jesus' perspective bring new light to the Sixth Commandment? Do you think equating hatred with murder is too strict?

How might temptation be used for good?

What underlying causes are fueling any destructive feelings within you? What will you do about it?

How does God want you to be building people up (including yourself) and not tearing them down?

If you would have
the nuptial union last,
let virtue be the bond
that ties it fast.

NICHOLAS ROWE

RULE VII

Follow God's Recipe for Intimacy

YOU SHALL NOT COMMIT ADULTERY.

EXODUS 20:14

I was a single college student and I found him very attractive. He was several years older than I, and I appreciated hearing his perspective on issues. Each day during our break from philosophy class, we would stand talking outside the classroom at the end of the hall that faced the ocean. He was even-tempered but also had a ready laugh. I kept waiting for him to ask me out for a date, yet the invitation never came.

Then one day, as we stood talking, I looked down and noticed he wore a wedding ring. "It wasn't there before," I thought. "Oh, rats!"

Laughing slightly, I pointed to his ring. "How did that happen? Did you get married over the weekend?"

He looked down at his ring and frowned slightly. I don't remember if he looked at me or continued to stare at his ring, but I'll never forget what he said next, even though it was over thirty-two years ago. He said softly, "I didn't like what my wife was doing, so I hadn't been wearing it."

Several years later, when I got married, I promised to be faithful to my husband, Larry. To me, part of what that means is always wearing my wedding ring.

Whatever your personal convictions are about wearing your wedding ring, the issue is a small one in comparison to the many commitments we make in marriage and the many responsibilities we take on when we say "I do." At the marriage altar we are promising to remain faithful both with our hearts and our bodies. "Marriage should be honored by all, and the marriage bed kept pure, for God will judge the adulterer and all the sexually immoral" (Hebrews 13:4).

The Wonders of Marriage

God designed marriage to be the most wonderful thing we could ever experience—apart from our relationship with Him. In fact, He describes marriage as representing our spiritual relationship with Him and calls Christians His "Bride." Our faithfulness in marriage should reflect God's faithfulness to His people.

Of course, we know none of our marriages is perfect, but God does want us to celebrate the wonders, even the mysteries, of marriage. Larry and I weren't always best friends and didn't appreciate God's gift of marriage, but now we wouldn't trade it for the world. We are best friends. We look to each other for companionship, knowing there's nothing we can't share with each other. And if I had a choice, I would elect to be with Larry over anyone else in the world.

Another benefit is support. When I need help, I know Larry and I can work on a problem or challenge together. Two heads really are better than one. We depend on each other to bring a different perspective than our own. We each have areas of expertise that we value in the other. Whether it's about disciplining the children, or talking over a decision we need to make, we recognize the value our combined outlook.

A spiritual bond is a wonderful aspect of marriage. We are so grateful that we both serve the same Lord and want His will to be done. Whether we're praying together, going to church together, or sharing what God has done in our lives, we have the same basic focus in life: bring glory to God.

Last, but certainly not least, the joy of sex is a delightful aspect of our relationship. Through our sexual intimacy, we have fun and share passion, and even use it as a way of appreciating each other through attention and pleasure. We know that sex is the one activity that will never be shared with anyone else while we both live. We can look at each other with a knowing nod that no one else can share. And no one else knows how to please us like we have learned to do for each other.

Is our marriage perfect? Of course not. We have disagreements and at times, I want to break Rule 7. But our marriage is the best example of God's work in our lives that I know of.

Singularly God's

Does this mean the seventh rule isn't for single people? No, I think its principles can be applied to singles as well. For example, the purity that this commandment stresses within marriage applies to the chastity God wants for people who are not married. Although marriage is a wonderful joy, I've met singles who were completely satisfied in their position and handled their sexual desires well. I've also been in contact with those who hungrily desire to be married, thinking a spouse will bring contentment. But marriage in itself doesn't bring contentment.

We must be joyful and happy about ourselves first, otherwise marriage will only bring great stress to a bridge that is already cracked.

I've also met singles who aren't handling their sexuality in a godly manner. They are not being "singularly God's." They experience temporary pleasures, but they do not have the deep joy of knowing and following God.

God isn't withholding something good from singles when He prohibits them from sex. He is their spouse and wants them be undividedly devoted to Him, unhindered by unhealthy sexual unions. Each sexual union takes a part of the single person's being. God wants single people to be pure so that all their being can be devoted to Him and if He desires them to experience marriage in the future, they won't bring sexual baggage into that union.

Pastor and author Bill Hybels writes, "It is impossible to walk away from sex unchanged, for sex is, by definition, the giving of the essence of oneself to another person. In sex outside marriage, you leave part of yourself with that sexual partner. You no longer feel whole."[1]

Sex: A Project in Intimacy

When we expose our bodies in lovemaking with a husband or wife, we lay bare all of our inadequacies. When we engage in passion we are lowering our protective walls. As we risk being out of control with delight, we are saying, "Will you still love me after you see me without my guard up?"

David A. Seamands writes, "Sex is the most tangible way we can give our love to someone. It involves much more than our bodies. During sex we give our most precious, private feelings. We offer the essence of our personality. When we engage in sex with someone other than our mates we trample upon velvet feelings and sensitivities. The adulterer is misusing another person."[2]

The Hebrew word used in the Bible for *sex* is *yada*, which can also be translated as our verb *to know*. In other words, according to scripture, to have sex with a person is to know that person. Additionally, *yada* communicated the ideas of loving, valuing, and caring for another person without shielding him or her from any part of oneself.

Liz Curtis Higgs writes, "As kids, we giggled when adults said of someone, 'He knew her, in the biblical sense,' and raised their eyebrows as they said it. I wasn't sure what that kind of 'knowing' was, but it sounded like pretty powerful stuff.

"It is. The word *know* here means that very thing: to have the most intimate understanding of someone. That is how God knows us, completely naked, able to hide nothing from him. I blush at the thought of it."[3]

Before the Fall Adam and Eve were "naked and felt no shame" (Genesis 2:25). After sinning, however, "they realized they were naked; so they sewed fig leaves together and made coverings for themselves" (Genesis 3:7). Take note of this. Their first reaction to sinning was to hide a part of themselves from each other. They were no longer innocently vulnerable with each other.

Bill Hybels also addresses that innocence: "The intimacy Adam and Eve shared before the Fall must have been wonderful, more wonderful than intimacy has been ever since, unhindered as it was by the self-serving nature of sin. But we must make love in a fallen world. As sinners we can never fully enjoy the gift but are always destined to distort it, deflecting some of its power into dangerous and destructive paths."[4]

There is no greater joy than that which comes from being accepted unconditionally after revealing oneself absolutely. That is why God speaks so highly of sex in all of Scripture. His Word encourages sex in the right context of marriage. One of the greatest Christian thinkers of the twentieth century, C. S. Lewis, said, "I know some muddle-headed Christians have talked as if Christianity thought that sex, or the body, or pleasure, were bad in themselves. But they were wrong. . . . Christianity has glorified marriage more than any other religion: and nearly all the greatest love poetry in the world has been produced by Christians."[5]

Here are some relevant passages from scripture:

May your fountain be blessed, and may you rejoice in the wife of your youth. A loving doe, a graceful deer—may her breasts satisfy you always, may you ever be captivated by her love. (Proverbs 5:18–19)

Enjoy life with your wife, whom you love, all the days of this meaningless life that God has given you under the sun—all your meaningless days. For this is your lot in life and in your toilsome labor under the sun. (Ecclesiastes 9:9)

Let him kiss me with the kisses of his mouth—for your love is more delightful than wine. (Song of Songs 1:2)

Like an apple tree among the trees of the forest is my lover among the young men. I delight to sit in his shade, and his fruit is sweet to my taste. He has taken me to the banquet hall, and his banner over me is love. Strengthen me with raisins, refresh me with apples, for I am faint with love. His left arm is under my head, and his right arm embraces me. (Song of Songs 2:3–6)

Your neck is like the tower of David, built with elegance; on it hang a thousand shields, all of them shields of warriors. Your two breasts are like two fawns, like twin fawns of a gazelle that browse among the lilies. (Song of Songs 4:4–5)

The husband should fulfill his marital duty to his wife, and likewise the wife to her husband. The wife's body does not belong to her alone but also to her husband. In the same way, the husband's body does not belong to him alone but also to his wife. Do not deprive each other except by mutual consent and for a time, so that you may devote yourselves to prayer. Then come together again so that Satan will not tempt you because of your lack of self-control. (1 Corinthians 7:3–5)

The beautiful things God's Word says about sex reflect the way God intended sexual union to be. God created sex for a married couple's pleasure, and He wants us to enjoy it. Sharing ourselves with someone other than our spouses, either in sexual union or an emotional affair, spoils the joy of married love.

Adultery

When people commit adultery, they hurt their spouses certainly, but they also do terrible damage to themselves. "Flee from sexual immorality. All other sins a man commits are outside his body, but he who sins sexually sins against his own body" (I Corinthians 6:18).

Dr. Kathryn Presley, a college professor, told me, "Aside from its far-reaching effects, breaking the Seventh Commandment seems often to carry with it intense guilt, which always separates us from God. I've learned over the decades to spot those young women in my Sunday School classes who are guilt-ridden over abortion, adultery, or other sexual sins. It is very difficult for them to accept God's grace and forgiveness."

God has written a personal moral code on our hearts, and even without spiritual training, upon breaking such a code people can sense the loss of their purity. That's why a child who is the victim of sexual abuse knows something is wrong, even though the perpetrator will try to convince the child that it is fun or loving. The child recoils at how his or her body is being used, even if the child has never attended Sunday School.

Adultery, or sex outside marriage for singles, is the violation of that inner moral code and lowers one's opinion of oneself.

Adultery, and the divorce that often results, hurts the children of the union. When one couple tried to tell their children as carefully as possible that they were getting a divorce, their young daughter burst into tears and cried out, "I promise to be good, Daddy!"

Children interpret their parents' difficulties as a reflection of their own inadequacies. I've talked to so many people, especially women, who remember praying to God when their parents were fighting about adultery, "God, I promise to be good if Mommy and Daddy won't get a divorce." When the divorce occurs, children can easily develop perfectionistic tendencies out of a need to control the uncontrollable spin of their lives. Being "good enough" seems like the way to right their upsidedown world. If they can perform perfectly, maybe mommy and daddy will be reunited again.

Pastor Gary Richmond, author of the book *The Divorce Decision*, writes, "Children have a dream to which they are entitled—at least in childhood. This dream we call 'And they lived happily ever after.' It has everything to do with how they view their future. If they gain the view that their future is uncertain and unpredictable, their lives will manifest several disastrous symptoms."[6]

Pastor Richmond says children of divorce are more likely to spend time in jail, experience mental and physical problems, and their marriages are at greater risk of failing.[7]

In *Campus Life* magazine Jim Burns responds to letters from readers in his "Let's Talk" column. He received this letter: "I think about my youth leader all the time, and go to youth group so I can be near him. I have a crush on him, even though he's married. I talk to him about my problems and he always understands and helps. I get very depressed when a week goes by that I don't see him. Since my own father deserted my mom and me when I was seven, I think my youth leader is the dad I never had. I'm confused. What do you think I should do?"

Besides giving helpful advice, Jim Burns points out, "I think you are very wise to have figured out that your crush on your youth leader probably has something to do with your absent father. Many young women who haven't had a father around while they're growing up, do struggle in their relationships with men. Often they try desperately to replace the love they never received from their dad."[8]

Thankfully, regardless of the destruction adultery causes, God has grace enough to forgive every sin, including adultery. God's plan is for the good of His children, and whenever any law or intention of His is broken, no matter how grievously, He offers His forgiveness. This is never more apparent than in Jesus' response to the woman caught in adultery. After confronting the sinfulness of the men who brought her to Him, even though Leviticus 20:10 required her to be stoned to death, Jesus said to her, "Woman, where are they? Has no one condemned you?" When she said, "No one," He replied, "Then neither do I condemn you. . . . Go now and leave your life of sin" (John 8:10–11).

Max Lucado writes about Jesus' words to that woman saying, "If you have ever wondered how God reacts when you fail, frame these words and hang them on the wall. Read them. Ponder them. Drink from them. Stand below them and let them wash over your soul."[9]

If you are like that woman, know that you too are not condemned if you've come to Jesus for His forgiveness. There is no sin that cannot be cleansed through His blood shed on the cross. Romans 8:1–2 assures us, "Therefore, there is now no condemnation for those who are in Christ Jesus, because through Christ Jesus the law of the Spirit of life set me free from the law of sin and death."

The World's Recipe

Several years ago when former President Jimmy Carter expressed honestly his lustful thoughts, many people snickered because they didn't think having lustful thoughts was sin. Yet, Jesus said not only is the act of adultery wrong but even thoughts about it. "You have heard that it was said, 'Do not commit adultery.' But I tell you that anyone who looks at a woman lustfully has already committed adultery with her in his heart. If your right eye causes you to sin, gouge it out and throw it away. It is better for you to lose one part of your body than for your whole body to be thrown into hell. And if your right hand causes you to sin, cut it off and throw it away. It is better for you to lose one part of your body than for your whole body to go into hell" (Matthew 5:27–30).

Jesus is not saying an initial glance is sinful; dwelling on it is. R. Kent Hughes writes, "Jesus forbids the second look. Generally, one is not responsible for the first look. But culpability begins with the repeated look, the stare, the libidinous leer. . . . He forbids mental musings that would be immoral if acted out."[10]

In contrast, the world says such fantasizing is perfectly all right, and the result is that many are caught up into thoughts that put them at the edge of the slippery cliff of adultery. The Internet is the current vehicle Satan uses to push people to the edge of this cliff while at the time they don't know they are headed for destruction.

In an Ann Landers column in the *LA Times*, a reader writes about the subject of how the Internet is affecting marriages. He had only been on line for a month yet was spending five hours a day engrossed in net surfing. He lists all the advantages he finds through the Internet and then writes, "Perhaps the reason these marriages are breaking up (as mine will soon) is because the computer-literate person has finally found something infinitely more interesting than the person he is married to."[11]

The world says, "If you're dissatisfied in your marriage, find whatever will meet your needs," but Jesus' words warn that putting your affections elsewhere than your marriage is wrong. He says to cut off "the right hand" if it is contributing to sin. He's referring to the spiritual removal of any harmful practices that will contribute to our hearts being pulled away from any right commitments we've made. That could mean limiting Internet surfing so that our spouses can be given the attention they need. It could mean turning off the television so that a couple can go out on a date. It could mean saying no to the invitation for lunch from a co-worker of the opposite sex.

Make a Decision to Love

When it seems like everything else, even on-line chats, will meet our needs better than a husband or wife, we need to make a decision to love that is not based on our feelings. Just as it is a choice to love our parents, it is also a choice to love our spouses.

After sharing that concept at a women's retreat, Martha shared with me that it had struck a chord with her. She believed she hated Jonathan, her husband, and admitted becoming very friendly with a man in her church. "Dan and I are just friends," she tried to assure me, but her lowered eyes confessed what her lips couldn't. "OK," she whispered, "I've been wondering whether we are becoming soul mates. He is such a good listener and is always giving me such godly advice. He even tells me how to respond to my husband, but I don't want to because then I will lose the closeness with Dan."

We talked longer and by the time we ended our conversation, she seemed willing to try to make a decision to love Jonathan. I heard from her some time later through email and she wrote, "Well, I did it. I couldn't say 'I love you' out loud, but I did look at him and think it. I've also told Dan we can't talk privately any more. My heart just about broke to tell him, but I know I've got to do the right thing. My own parents divorced over my father's unfaithfulness and I can see now I was headed in that direction too. I find that really ironic since I swore as a child that I'd never do to my kids what my father did to us kids."

Several weeks later, Martha gave me another update. "I finally realized that one of the reasons I couldn't love Jonathan is because he has a heart problem. I was afraid that if I fell back in love with him, he'd die and leave me alone with all those loving feelings. I didn't realize that I was unconsciously protecting myself from potential grief by staying emotionally separated. Now I am more willing to risk. The other night I still hadn't been able to say 'I love you' out loud, but before he came to bed, I patted his pillow and whispered it. I think I'm getting closer."

Martha has come a long way from standing at the edge of that slippery cliff. She has turned around and begun walking the other way. Here are some other ways to make that turn away from adultery:

Realize that you can make that decision to love even if you don't *like* your spouse right now. Clint wrote me saying, "There are times when I don't like what my wife does or says, but I try to remember God doesn't like what I do or say all the time either. But He doesn't stop loving me—after all, He saved me in spite of who I am. I am also commanded to *love*, but I haven't found a verse yet that commands me to *like*. It isn't possible for me to like everyone, I'm not wired that way. But it is possible for me to love everyone when I draw upon the Holy Spirit's power."

Another way to come to a decision to love is to focus on the positives of how God is using a spouse to create greater godliness in us. Corrine told me, "I believe that God brings spouses together to bring us to the cross. If we can look to God during a disagreement instead of being mad at our spouses, then Jesus is able to deal with our hurts and old patterns of behavior.

Our spouses can be used by God to grind down the hard and rough edges within us so that we can be in right relationship with Him and our spouses."

That's what the Bible talks about in Genesis 2:18, "The Lord God said, 'It is not good for the man to be alone. I will make a helper suitable for him.'" Interestingly, before the creation of Eve, God presented all of the animals to Adam but none was the "the suitable helper." Adam needed this experience before God introduced him to woman.

When you think of "suitable," think of a suit, fitted by a tailor to complement all the different parts of his body. The idea is where he lacks, she supplies, and where she lacks, he supplies. The differences of our spouses are meant to complement us, but it is easy to think negatively about them. Be careful. If we think too negatively about them for too long, we run the risk of falling for Satan's lie that we need to find someone else who will meet our needs. Satan sniffs and smells a needy heart and dangles before it the carrot of adultery.

Seeing the benefits of our mate's personality and perspective can help us to resist that carrot. For instance, if you lack assertiveness and your spouse is decisive, recognize how that quality can encourage your growth rather than thinking your spouse is too aggressive. If you have lots of energy and look down on your spouse as lazy, perhaps it would be a good idea to adjust your thinking to appreciate how your spouse enjoys life at a more leisurely pace. If you think your wife needs to be more strict in disciplining your children, consider that maybe you are too strict. His or her influence could help you to be less perfectionistic in your expectations.

Making a decision to love by expressing it verbally and then by appreciating your spouse's differences will strengthen you to obey the Seventh Commandment.

Meet Your Mate's Needs

The ultimate challenge we'll face in keeping the Seventh Commandment is to meet the needs of our spouse, even if he or she doesn't make an effort to meet our needs. Ideally, God wants every husband and wife to meet the needs of his or her spouse, while realizing that only God can meet all our needs. He did give us the key for identifying those needs and meeting them in Ephesians. "However, each one of you also must love his wife as he loves himself, and the wife must respect her husband" (Ephesians 5:33).

Do you remember in the first chapter when I mentioned Dr. Larry Crabb's insights about the needs of men and women? Women primarily need security, which can be defined as unconditional love. Men essentially need significance, which comes with feeling respected. I can certainly see the connection to Ephesians 5:33. Can you? Understanding those needs and seeking to meet them may prevent our mates from succumbing to the lure of adultery. Is that a guarantee? No, because every person makes his or her own choices. Am I responsible if my mate succumbs? No, because each person is responsible for the decisions he or she makes. Edith Schaeffer wrote, "'To avoid having your children steal buns from the bakery, have fresh baked buns waiting for them at home after school.' It is the same kind of practical warning that if marriage is indeed to help people stay away from immorality, then there should be a responsibility taken by each of the two to fulfill each other's needs as much as possible."[12]

A love for sexual intimacy will go far in helping a mate—and ourselves—to resist adultery. Many women and some men complain that their spouse is just too interested in sex. But I often say, "If you haven't eaten all day, what do you concentrate on?" Eating, of course. Well, for those who are starving sexually, they aren't able to concentrate on anything other than that. Meet that need and you may find your spouse thinking of other things.

Companionship is another important aspect of meeting needs. Larry likes nothing better than for me to rub his feet while he's watching Monday night football on TV. Although that has no value to me, I do it anyway. He makes the choice of taking me out to dinner frequently. We're both happy and each of us has sacrificed little.

Meeting the emotional needs of our mates is another important aspect of resisting adultery. A man's need for respect is met through the admiration his wife gives. Does she compliment him in his abilities? Does she speak highly of him to others? Does she listen and not interrupt? Does she praise the help he gives around the house even though it's done in a different style than she would do it?

Does a husband listen with his eyes, not just his ears? Does he refrain from giving advice until his wife asks for it? Does he value the trip and not just the arrival on their vacation? Does he consider his wife's opinion important even though he may think he already knows the decision they should make?

All these little things add up to creating an atmosphere of love and respect. When your spouse senses that you are being selfless with a cheerful attitude, she or he can't help but respond. Yes, some may not, and then we'll need a greater portion of God's strength to know we are pleasing Him even if we aren't pleasing our spouses. Our fundamental goal should be to please our Lord who sacrificed so much for us.

Twenty years ago, Muriel McQuilken showed signs of Alzheimer's disease and now is not able to speak or care for any of her own needs. After almost fifty years of marriage, Muriel's husband Robertson resigned his position as president of Columbia International University to care for his wife. As exhilarating as his work had been, he says he has enjoyed learning to cook and keep house, although some have called him foolish for caring for someone who doesn't even know he's sacrificing for her.

At one point of frustration, Robertson asked God why he'd been pulled out of his beloved work. He asked, "Father, I like this assignment, and I have no regrets. But if a coach puts a man on the bench, he must not want him in the game. You needn't tell me, of course, but I'd like to know—why didn't you need me in the game?"

Robertson didn't sleep well that night and awoke contemplating the puzzle. Muriel was still mobile at that time, so they set out on their morning walk around the block. Muriel wasn't too sure on her feet, so they went slowly and held hands as they always did. That day Robertson heard footsteps behind them and looked back to see the familiar form of a local bum. He staggered past them, then turned and looked them up and down. "Tha's good. I likes 'at," he said. "Tha's real good. I likes it."

The small man turned and headed back down the street, mumbling to himself over and over, "Tha's good. I likes it."

When Muriel and Robertson reached their garden and sat down, the man's words came back to Robertson. Then the realization hit him; the Lord had spoken through an inebriated old derelict. "It is you who are whispering to my spirit, 'I likes it, tha's good,'" Robertson said aloud to God. "I may be on the bench, but if you like it and say it's good, that's all that counts."[13]

God is saying to you "I like that" when you meet the needs of your beloved even though you don't agree with everything he or she does. God likes it when you give unconditional love— even if only in obedience to Him. God likes it when you bat away the carrot of adultery that Satan dangles in front of you when you're hurt or disgusted about your spouse's actions or lack of attention. Even if you never see your sacrifice of keeping your promise of purity rewarded on earth, God has taken it into account.

Search Yourself

What do you find interesting about the creation of
Eve for Adam?

❧

Which of the reasons for which God established
marriage is important to you?

❧

Do you find it easy or difficult to think of sexual
intimacy as God's gift?

❧

What similarities do you see between idolatry and
adultery?

❧

In what ways does Satan hint that adultery will
meet a person's needs?

❧

If you need to make a decision to love your spouse,
how and when will you do that?

A wrongdoer is often a man who has left something undone, not always one who has done something.

MARCUS AURELIUS
ANTONINUS

RULE VIII

Never Steal, but Forever Give

YOU SHALL NOT STEAL.

EXODUS 20:15

One day in December, 1998, Conrad Buchanan was working as a security guard at a Ventura, California mall. He happened to look up and see a woman perched on the edge of the parking garage—six stories up. He couldn't believe it, but she seemed like she was going to jump off.

His heart beat wildly with horror as she left the edge, plummeting through the air. Conrad ran toward the woman and placed himself under her. Extending his arms, he tried to catch the suicidal woman. She crashed into him and they both hit the ground.

When Conrad became conscious again, he couldn't move. By blocking the woman's fall, he paid the price of a broken neck and became a quadriplegic. The woman later died, but Conrad says he does not regret his choice even though he will never walk again.

What is Conrad's story doing in a chapter about the Eighth Commandment? Stealing is not just taking something that is not ours; stealing is also withholding something good from someone besides ourselves. Conrad endangered his own life to try to give something good to that hopeless woman: life. He didn't steal from her something he could offer, an opportunity to reconsider her choice.

One may be tempted to think Conrad was foolish because the end result of his bravery was the death of the woman and his own paralysis, but consider the alternative. What if he had seen her jump and just stood there watching her fall, knowing he could at least get between her and the ground? Imagine the sound. Imagine the sight. And now imagine the memories Conrad would likely have to cope with for the rest of life. Imagine how the "What if?" question would assault his psyche for at least a very long time. With such consequences for cowardice, is there any room left to doubt that Conrad did the right thing?

Who Me? Steal?

Most of us know what stealing is and most of us don't consider ourselves thieves. Yet, God still needed to tell us all not to steal. That's because we are good at deceiving ourselves into defining theft as something extraordinary, conveniently forgetting the little ways we do indeed steal.

My stealing days go back to my preteen years. Days after I turned thirteen, I planned to go to the movies with some friends. The child's fare in those days (the 1960s) ended when a person turned thirteen. I didn't want to pay more money just because I had become a teenager, and so I devised a plan. Of course, I easily rationalized my plan. "After all," I told myself, "it's only been a few days since I was twelve. The theater has a lot of money anyway. No one will know. It's only fair, considering I don't have a job and will have to use my pitiful allowance. I'm not hurting anyone. I won't really be taking any *thing*! I'll pay the full price the next time!"

Even with all those mental gymnastics, I still felt crummy as I put my plan into action. I wore no makeup. I did my hair in a style I thought made me look younger. I wore clothes that I thought looked more immature, and I put on an innocent, childlike look. I marched up to the theater window and said, "One child's admission, please."

The teenager behind the glass took one look at me and said, "What year were you born?"

I wasn't ready for that! What year was I born? Nervous and guilty, I wound up giving an earlier year instead of a later one.

"Sorry, that makes you eligible for the adult rate." And she quoted the higher price!

"Rats!" I thought, humiliated.

I slinked into the theatre and mentally kicked myself throughout the movie. While my friends sat blissfully enjoying the movie looking like the cool teenagers they were, I sat there with my hair, face, and clothes looking dumber than dumb. I had finally arrived at the dignified position of being a teenager, yet I looked like a stupid twelve-year-old.

I'm grateful that God allowed me to suffer those consequences. There have been many times since that the memory of them has served as a good reminder. Like the time I realized out in the parking lot that the cashier had charged me too little for the broom I bought. I took it back and paid the difference. I also recognize the times I have withheld something that was due someone, like a promise. If I were honest with myself, I would acknowledge that I had effectively stolen something.

Paul writes to the Ephesians, "He who has been stealing must steal no longer, but must work, doing something useful with his own hands, that he may have something to share with those in need" (Ephesians 4:28). Evidently there were those who were keeping up their old line of work, thievery, even as believers.

Today, we can steal in ways that people might consider acceptable or as mere slips of forgetfulness:

- using copyrighted pictures or ideas from the Internet without giving credit
- copying material from books without written permission
- using songs for worship without written permission
- cheating on a test by copying someone's answers
- taking supplies home from work
- taking the hotel towel home in a suitcase
- being dishonest on our income tax form
- taking a book from the library and never returning it
- inadvertently taking the church's pew Bible home and never taking it back

We may have forgotten to write for permission or we may have intended to take the book back or we may have taken the towel by mistake, but unless we do something to make restitution, we are thieves. How easy it is to allow one slip to become another. Sooner or later, grand larceny doesn't seem so extraordinary. Author William Hendricks writes, "What we do in the small issues of life sets the stage for bigger issues. What we do at the copier, on the phone, in front of the mail machine are important and set the stage for how we will respond to greater temptations that *will come!* It is also true that once we violate our conscience in an area it is easier to do it the next time. Before long, our heart becomes callous."[1]

Why is it important to take *all* stealing seriously? Because we're not only stealing from our employer, the hotel management, or the store; we are actually stealing from God. Remember that God owns everything! "The earth is the Lord's, and everything in it, the world, and all who live in it; for he founded it upon the seas and established it upon the waters" (Psalm 24:1–2).

The Clenched Fist

Not only are we stealing from God when we take something that isn't ours, we are also stealing from God when we withhold good from someone or resist giving something that is rightfully due. Any thievery is the result of resisting God's lordship in our lives. Alan Redpath writes, ". . . every instance of theft can be traced to this source and can be found to be due to failure to submit to the control of the Holy Spirit in our personal lives."[2]

It's easy to rationalize one small theft, but when we look at it from God's perspective, we must admit that we have in that moment said to God, "No, God, you are not my Lord in this instance."

I'm convicted repeatedly as I remember withholding the protection of someone's property one day as I went out to my car after bowling. I noticed that a bowling bag had been left in the parking lot of the bowling alley. Evidently, someone had forgotten to put it into their car and drove away. I thought of the reasons I couldn't or rather didn't want to take the time to take the bag back inside. *I'm late to my hair appointment. Someone else will see it and take care of it. Am I my brother's keeper?*

I drove away.

I drove away!

It would have been so simple to do the good and caring thing, but I chose not to. In that moment I acted like a thief, for as Martin Luther said, "We should fear and love God that we may not take our neighbor's money or goods, but help him to improve and protect his property and business."[3]

Would I have ever considered stealing that bowling bag? Absolutely not! But I'd succumbed to another form of theft.

It's easy to do. We might sell our used car for more than its worth to an unsuspecting buyer or not tell him or her about a potential problem. We could refuse to give a raise to a deserving employee. We might park in a handicapped parking space. We might call in sick to work when we want to take a day off. We could withhold repaying a debt to a friend and use the money elsewhere.

As Billy Graham experienced, we might withhold care for the poor and needy. He writes, "I was riding with a wealthy man in the back seat of his chauffeur-driven Cadillac out to his home on Long Island. We passed along the edge of Harlem. I told him that a few days before I had made a tour of some of the poverty-stricken areas of Harlem and East Harlem. He shrugged his shoulders and said, 'That's something we don't think about.' If he were a Christian it would be his duty to think about it and do what he could about it. In a true sense we are our brothers' keepers. As Christians we are to be Good Samaritans."[4]

We could also be guilty of refusing to use the talents and abilities that God has given us to use for His glory. Or, we could refuse the Spirit's prompting to tell someone about the good news of Jesus.

Stealing isn't just taking something; it's refusing to give something that God wants us to give. When we think of it like that, we know God was thinking of us when He said, "Don't steal." Ouch! Now we're beginning to see how we routinely break one of God's top ten rules.

To Steal from Another Is to Steal from Oneself

Whether we steal in big or small ways, we never feel good about it. I didn't feel good about trying to deprive that theatre of its deserved money—and I've never forgotten it. Eva Marie wrote to tell me, "I stole a pencil once in the second grade. Obviously I never got over it!!!" Maybe you can remember an incident from your childhood. Maybe you can remember an incident of the more recent past.

Helen told me about the regret she felt when she withheld

her mother's precious Bible from her sister. She had promised it to her sister but kept telling herself she would give it to her the next time she saw her. She never did.

Helen says,

> Breaking my promise about that Bible ate at me for twelve years. It seemed to fuel the poor relationship between me and my sister. I couldn't stand the thought of letting the Bible go. My mom and I had a very close relationship, so I thought I should be the one to have her Bible. But God finally helped me realize that because my sister didn't have as close a relationship with Mom as I had, she needed the treasured keepsake even more.
>
> One day my sister and I made a lunch date. She came over and brought me a little gift. I had something for her too—our Mom's Bible. We both cried and hugged each other. She smiled at me in a way I had not seen for a long time. God brought us closer as I recognized I had been 'stealing' that Bible from its rightful owner.

When we steal, we carry the weight of a guilty conscience and miss the joy of a clean one. When we steal by not giving our all on the job, we miss the joy of working hard. When we withhold good from someone, we miss the rewards God intended to give us for our generosity and service.

Zacchaeus had carried a heavy heart for a long time until he encountered Jesus in Luke 19:2. After repenting of his sins, Zacchaeus knew he was forgiven. He then exclaimed he would repay those he had cheated. We can picture the relief and joy he experienced as he welcomed his Savior into his home. The home of his heart had been swept clean from the burden of theft it had carried for so long.

Author and speaker Patsy Clairmont describes Zacchaeus by writing, "That day he stepped down from his own efforts to see and be seen and stepped up to the call of the Lord. Zacchaeus still lacked inches, but he gained insight and walked away a giant of a man."[5]

God wants that to happen in our own lives. God desires to graciously forgive and cleanse us for breaking any of His rules. If we've stolen anything or withheld any kind of good from someone, God wants us to follow Zacchaeus's good example. We can be set free from the burden of the wrong choices we've made. We'll also be encouraged to keep giving what is due with a generous heart.

Hearty Work Heartily Done

We will reduce the temptation to steal as we dedicate every moment to the Lord, knowing that everything we do is an offering to Him. We are His servants and His representatives whether we are on the job, at home, shopping, or participating in sports. As each of us sees his or her being dedicated to Him, we'll resist the theft of time ill spent or the theft of doing only a lackluster job.

Ephesians 6:7–8 exhorts us, "Serve wholeheartedly, as if you were serving the Lord, not men, because you know that the Lord will reward everyone for whatever good he does, whether he is slave or free."

My sister Karen wrote her thoughts about working heartily for the Lord: "I think we steal from God and ourselves when we work for our own benefit at our jobs or in our businesses. If we work for ourselves, we become upset with our employees because they aren't promoting our reputation perfectly, or we worry because we think we must provide for ourselves. But if we can work focused on building the Kingdom of God, instead of the 'Kingdom of Karen,' we will be at rest and have increased satisfaction in our work."

Serving wholeheartedly, either as a homemaker, employer, employee, full-time Christian servant, or day laborer, ensures we won't steal by doing less than our best. Myrtie expressed that thought this way: "Resisting 'robbing God' means that one hundred percent of our being, time, energy, and money is committed to God so that we never take anything away from promoting His eternal plan."

David A. Seamands reminds us, "Stealing is getting the reward without paying the price, collecting the dividend without making the investment. . . . Our lives are an investment. Life involves putting something into it and receiving something in return. Stealing, however, is the shortcut philosophy of life that contradicts this basic principle of the universe."[6]

Jesus was willing to pay the complete price of giving His life for our restored relationship with the Father. We shouldn't cut corners as we represent Him.

Do What You Say and Say What You Mean

Failing to keep a promise or commitment could also be considered stealing. We might do that by:

- volunteering or agreeing to do more than we can possibly complete
- making an appointment that we don't intend to keep
- looking for the approval of others as the motivation for our activity

When we renege on a promise, or try to do too much and thus present an inferior product, we have stolen from those to whom we are rightfully indebted. We've taken a shortcut. Quality is the result of dedicating ourselves in complete commitment.

James 5:12 warns us, "Above all, my brothers, do not swear—not by heaven or by earth or by anything else. Let your 'Yes' be yes, and your 'No,' no, or you will be condemned."

Knowing that no matter what we do, we are serving God, we should only commit to those things that God wants us to do and not worry about what others think of us if we must say no. That's hard. Consider the insights of some who have said no at the right time:

SUZY: "I have a hard time saying no because I want others to like me. This has siphoned my energy and created stress in my life in the past. Now, before I give an answer, I pray and ask God what He thinks. He will never give me more than I can handle."

EVA MARIE: "I used to be the yes girl! I would say yes to things I knew I did not have time to do! In the end, I stole from God and my family to do them. Then, in 1992, I became very ill. Saying no was not an option, it was a necessity. As my illness stabilized, I found that the lessons I learned during that period gave me the strength to say things like, 'I would really love to help you on that, but I will have to say no. I'm so sorry, this is not a good time. Let me know if I can be of assistance to you in the future.'"

KURT: "I will say no when I know I cannot keep the commitment or obligation, and I will tell the requestor why, if necessary. I believe it is a greater wrong to say yes, knowing I can't keep my word, than to say no in humble admission of my limitations. It is a matter of keeping my integrity rather than maintaining my image."

MYRTIE: "God's Word takes a hard stand against the 'blame, denial, and explain' game. If I've chosen ahead of time to say no and don't feel a need to give an explanation, I won't make unrealistic promises. If someone pushes me with their 'you should or you could' words, I politely repeat no as many times as it takes for them to accept my commitment."

JOAN: "When I committed to doing something God didn't want me to do, I realized I had been stealing the Lord's time because that activity took me away from His purposes for me."

ROBIN: "When tempted to make an unrealistic promise, I remember what my very wise husband says, 'When you say yes to something, you automatically say no to something else.'"

What wise reminders! Committing only to those things God wants us to do will help us keep our promises. We will in this way be able to produce a result that doesn't steal from our resources to bear the image of God.

Sometimes Christians overcommit themselves in service to their churches. Myrtie told me about how one church successfully addressed the problem. The pastoral staff and elders determined that no one in the church would have more than one responsibility at a time, nor could anyone have the same responsibility for more than two years. Before taking on a new responsibility, each person had to take a break for at least one year. Myrtie says there was no burnout at that church and, overall, everyone was fairly happy with his or her amount of service.

These ideas will help us to be good stewards of our time and possessions. You and I will do what we say and say what we mean if we seek God's will at each step and only commit to that which we know we can do in God's power.

Tithing

We can steal from God by not obeying God's call for a tithe. Malachi 3:8–12 reads,

> "Will a man rob God? Yet you rob me."
> "But you ask, 'How do we rob you?'
> "In tithes and offerings. You are under a curse—the whole nation of you—because you are robbing me. Bring the whole tithe into the storehouse, that there may be food in my house. Test me in this," says the Lord Almighty, "and see if I will not throw open the floodgates of heaven and pour out so much blessing that you will not have room enough for it. I will prevent pests from devouring your crops, and the vines in your fields will not cast their fruit," says the Lord Almighty. "Then all the nations will call you blessed, for yours will be a delightful land," says the Lord Almighty.

We rob God when we don't give to Him financially so that His work can be accomplished to His glory. In giving, we are showing our dedication to Him. Does God need our tithe? No, because as we read before in Psalm 24:1, He actually owns everything already. But giving back to Him a portion of what He has given us is our reasonable service and is of more benefit to us. It gives us the opportunity to express our gratitude and praise—and we are usually rewarded abundantly. Kurt says, "I always remember it's not my money God wants (it's all His to begin with), but my heart. God is a far better investor than I will ever be, therefore I know investing in Him will bring greater interest than trying to invest in earthly delights."

Why do we try to steal from God when He can bless us with much more than we would ever make without Him? You and I have no power to make ourselves wealthy no matter how hard we work. It is all in God's power and sovereign control. Deuteronomy tells us, "You may say to yourself, 'My power and the strength of my hands have produced this wealth for me.' But remember the Lord your God, for it is he who gives you the ability to produce wealth, and so confirms his covenant, which he swore to your forefathers, as it is today."

Gloria, the owner of a store, told me, "As I desired the store to be busy today, God reminded me that it was not my money that was coming into the store, but His. I think we steal from God when we think that our provision is from ourselves and not from Him. But wealth is strictly from Him. We want to own what we receive instead of seeing ourselves as merely the receptors and stewards of His gifts. There is so much peace in knowing that I am not responsible to provide for myself and that I work only for Him. If we say we are responsible our own wealth, we are not acknowledging God's providence. We are stealing the glory and honor and acknowledgment due only to Him."

A Holy Vocation: Blessing People's Socks Off!

If the Eighth Commandment is telling us that when we steal, we are withholding respect from God and others, what is the flip side?

Perhaps Edith Schaeffer can shed some light on the subject. She applies the principle of allowing the poor to glean in the fields, as detailed in Deuteronomy 24:19–22, to our modern lives by saying, "You may say, 'I don't have a field,' and feel that there is no possible application of this gleaning in your life. It seems to me we need to try to translate something of this into all of our lives. For me, leaving something in the corner of the fields, or a few grapes on the vines can be a larger than necessary tip to a weary-looking waitress, or a taxi driver who isn't expecting it, or a man lugging bags on the station platform, one on his shoulder, balancing the others in his hands."[7]

We may not even be able to speak Jesus' name to them, but God can use it. Maybe that waitress prayed that very morning for a few extra dollars to meet a financial need. We become the answer to her prayer.

We can also respect the rights of others by treating people the way we would want to be treated. We can smile instead of frown while in a crowd of people. We can greet the grocery clerk by name or give up our seat on a plane so that relatives can sit together. Anything that makes someone feel respected will guarantee that we haven't stolen the inherent respect they deserve as created beings of our loving God.

Conrad Buchanan showed that kind of respect when he tried to save the life of that woman who plummeted to her death. He tried to prevent her from robbing herself of life.

This same sacrificial respect for God's created beings was demonstrated after the crash of flight 1420 in Little Rock, Arkansas, in May, 1999. A band of twenty-five members from Ouachita Baptist University Choir aboard the plane risked their lives saving others because they, like Conrad Buchanan, didn't want to withhold life from others. They were returning from a choir tour in Europe and had already generously given of themselves to the people of Kosovo through song. On their way home, their plane skidded and burst into flames, landing in a horrible rain storm. Charles Colson reports that Barrett Barber, a 19-year-old minister's son, lifted passengers through a hole in the plane above an emergency exit that would not open. Choir member Luke Hollingsworth escaped from the tail section only to go back to help wounded passengers escape. On his own shoulders, the young man carried a woman with a broken pelvis across chest-deep water to safety. Choir director Charles Fuller got his wife out, then went back into the burning plane to help rescue an 80-year-old man with a broken hip. He was later seen guiding other passengers out of the fuselage onto the wing of the plane.

The acts of heroism didn't end even after the young people had gotten survivors off the plane. Rain and huge balls of hail were pelting down on injured passengers lying on the ground. Choir members huddled over them, using their own bodies as human shields against the hail and rain. They even took off their shirts to form makeshift blankets for the injured.

The heroism did not come without a price. Choir member James Harrison repeatedly ran back into the burning plane to pull passengers to safety. He was apparently overcome by smoke and collapsed. A few days ago, James's friends gathered at First Baptist Church of Royal, Arkansas, to bury Charles Wright, the head of Ouachita's music program, and quoted the words of James's Savior: "Greater love hath no man than this, that a man lay down his life for his friends."[8]

Though you and I may never have the challenge of saving a life, we can obey God's command not to steal by making sure we don't take anything that isn't ours and by making it our vocation to bless people's socks off!

Search Yourself

In the past, how have you seen people steal? Have you done any of the same things?

❊

Are you surprised to find that stealing also includes withholding that which is rightfully due to another? In what ways have you participated in this?

❊

How does God want you to work heartily for Him in the responsibilities He's given you?

❊

How can you make your "no" be "no" and your "yes" be "yes"?

❊

If you tithe, what motivates you to do so, and if you don't, what prevents you?

❊

How will you show respect for others today?

Truth exists,
only falsehood
has to be invented.

GEORGES BRAQUE

RULE
IX

Tell the Truth, the Whole Truth, and Nothing but the Truth

YOU SHALL NOT GIVE FALSE TESTIMONY
AGAINST YOUR NEIGHBOR.

EXODUS 20:16

It was third grade. Mrs. Leighton was my favorite teacher of all my student life and I was her favorite student of some thirty years of teaching (or at least I liked to think so). I was generally an honest person, but on one particular occasion I told a classmate something I knew wasn't true. When it was reported, Mrs. Leighton called on me and said, "I know Kathy will tell the truth. Kathy, what happened?"

The lie would keep me in the good graces of Mrs. Leighton and the truth would benefit my classmates. I went for Mrs. Leighton's approval and repeated the lie.

I can still remember the confident grin on my favorite teacher's face, and I can still remember the frown of rebuke on my classmates' faces. And I still remember the shame.

Many of us can feel the shame of a lie we told last week or last year. Lying is something we all do at one point or another, so it's no wonder that God had to include this prohibition in His rule book.

The Truth about Truth

From the translated wording of this commandment, "You shall not give false testimony against your neighbor" (Exodus 20:16), it might appear as though God were only commanding us to give a correct report within the court setting. But that isn't the only application. In fact, if that had been the case, scholars say that the wording in Hebrew at the beginning of the command would have been *Lo ta-eed*, meaning "Don't *testify* falsely against your neighbor." The actual Hebrew text in the Torah uses the phrase *Lo ta-ahneh*, which means "Don't answer, respond, or repeat against your neighbor."[1] Such wording certainly broadens the commandment's application.

Regardless of the intent, we know God wants us to be honest people because He's an honest God. He is the very essence of truthfulness. When teaching a class of youngsters, David A. Seamands asked, "What are some of the things God cannot do?"

Of course, the children looked at him with surprise. "God can do *anything*!" they responded.

Pastor Seamands queried, "Can He? Can He lie?" The children knew He couldn't do that, and after discussing it, they all recognized that God also can't share His glory with anyone or violate human freedom. Plus, he can't tolerate sin.[2]

The truthfulness that is woven intricately into God's nature is stressed throughout Scripture. Jesus said, "I am the way and *the truth* and the life. No one comes to the Father except through me" (John 14:6, italics mine). The Holy Spirit is described as the Spirit of Truth in John 14:17. Proverbs 6:16–17 tells us that a lying tongue are among the seven things God hates.

Eva Marie shared an important reminder with me when she said, "If God created the heavens and the earth by His words, then words are pretty powerful! There are countless Scripture verses about our words and our tongue. I believe that we must weigh each and every word that comes out of our mouths and make them honest."

God's words created everything and His words are always truthful. If we despise truth, we despise God because there isn't a dishonest bone in His figurative body.

The Father of Lies

In stark contrast to God's character of truth, Satan, God's enemy, is totally evil and inexhaustibly dishonest. His dependence on lies started when he thought he could be victorious in his rebellion against God. The first thing he said to a human (Eve) was a lie when he hissed, "Did God really say . . . ?" He continues today by whispering lies that you and I hear hundreds of times each day. And some of these whispers suggest that we lie too! Satan is the father of lies as Jesus identified him in John 8:44. Nothing, absolutely nothing, he tells us is to be believed as truth. And yet we succumb to his urgings every time we tell a lie.

We lie:

- by being silent when we should defend someone
- by passing along a tasty bit of gossip

- by exaggerating to make our story a little bit more entertaining
- by being prejudiced against a certain nationality
- by giving false information about someone for our own benefit
- by using the truth in a way that makes someone appear badly

Imagine what our world or society would be like if everyone told truth? Of course, that was the theme of Jim Carrey's movie, *Liar, Liar,* which hilariously revealed how lies influence our world every single day. I'm guilty of it. You're guilty of it. And we're guilty of rationalizing it by disguising it with other names like "tactfulness" or "little white lies" or saying, "I can't hurt their feelings."

We participate in lies when we listen to gossip or accept something before verifying its truthfulness. Gossip isn't always about something untruthful. It could be a delicious piece of truth passed along with the intention of hurting someone or damaging their reputation. Even exaggerating about someone could be detrimental.

Be careful not to exaggerate the truth, for this too is a kind of lying. We should listen to Patsy Clairmont when she says, "I've learned that less sometimes is more. This is not an easy lesson for my exaggeration-prone personality type."[3]

Thomas à Kempis, in *The Imitation of Christ,* said: "Be hesitant to believe the things you hear. Don't be quick to pour it into another's ears."[4]

Why Do We Lie Anyway?

If we can understand why we lie, we may be able to follow the ninth rule more faithfully.

One of the first reasons we lie is to defend ourselves. Darrell began lying to protect himself from the academic failure he experienced because of an unidentified and untreated learning disability. Because he didn't want to turn in an uncompleted homework assignment, and felt too stupid to ask for help, he would come up with excuses to delay turning it in. Of course, this didn't solve the problem, so Darrell had to concoct more tales to get out of doing homework. But it began a lifestyle of coping by lying.

In a similar way, I found that lying to myself about my abusive reactions toward my two-year-old daughter gave me a sense of false hope. After an outburst, I would promise myself, "I'll never hit her again," or "I'll stop yelling." For both Darrell and I, these defense mechanisms didn't work, but in the midst of pain, we humans will try anything to get rid of the hurt or confusion.

Pride is another cause that is often at the core of lying. We might exaggerate our academic accomplishments because we want to impress people. We've all seen news reports about "doctors" who were treating people and yet weren't trained or certified doctors at all—a prideful sham.

Gossiping is a form of lying that has many possible causes. We may feel important because we have some juicy tidbit and everyone's listening to us. We could also be trying to elevate our own reputation by tearing down someone else's.

Our motive could even be one of seeming love if we "gossip" in the form of giving a prayer request. It seems so noble to say, "Stan is really struggling again with his drug addiction. Let's pray for him." Yet, Stan may not have wanted that information shared with two hundred people through the prayer chain.

Robin wrote me saying, "Gossiping can be as innocuous as agreeing with a friend over a cup of tea that your husbands are both attracted to a certain part of a woman's anatomy. You have just betrayed your husband in an effort to bond with someone and feel comforted by someone else's experience or struggle."

Another form of lying is flattery. Someone has defined this as saying things to a person's face that you would never say behind his or her back. We may be trying to get ahead in our company or making sure we don't anger someone.

No matter what gives rise to them, our lies hurt ourselves and others. Be aware of the many different reason for lying, and you will be less likely to fall into temptation.

Exceptions to the General Rule

How far should our definition of lying go? Should we never withhold information? What if the truth will hurt someone's feelings? What about those midwives at the time of the birth of Moses who disobeyed the Pharaoh's command to kill all the male babies born to the Israelite mothers (Exodus 1:17)? Not only did they disobey, they lied and said they could never arrive at the birth on time to complete the dastardly deed (Exodus 1:19). What about the harlot, Rahab, who lied in order to protect the spies who were hiding on top of her roof (Joshua 2:5–6)? How about modern Christian heroes like Corrie ten Boom and her family, who lied to protect the Jews hidden in their home?

J. I. Packer refers to such examples and writes, "But does that square with the ninth commandment? In principle, yes. What is forbidden is false witness against your neighbor—that is, as we said, prideful lying designed to do him down, and exalt you at his expense. The positive command implicit in this negative is that we should seek our neighbor's good, and speak truth to him and about him to this end. When the love which seeks his good prompts us to withhold truth which, if spoken, would bring him harm, the spirit of the ninth commandments is being observed."[5]

That takes care of the oft-quoted trick question, "What would you do if your neighbor comes to your door asking for his wife, threatening to kill her—and she is hiding in your closet? Would you tell the truth or lie?"

The ultimate aim of any of God's rules is love.

That's why Marie's choice to "lie" to her daughter about a

sick kitten was right. She and Kelly, her six-year-old daughter, had found a kitten that wasn't able to see because of a horrible amount of mucus in his eyes. That evening, little Kelly prayed heartily for the kitten to be healed. After her daughter went to school the next day, Marie took the kitten to the vet and found out the animal had a disease that had already blinded it. The vet recommended the kitten be put down. In great sadness, Marie agreed.

When Kelly returned home from school that day, she immediately asked about the kitten. "Can he see now?"

"Yes," Marie replied. "He can see now."

"Will he come to live with us?" she asked.

"No," Marie answered. "Someone else wanted him, so I said okay."

Marie says, "It was a twist on the truth. Some would call it a lie. But my daughter was so young and I didn't want to break her heart."

Marie acted in love.

Guigo I, a Carthusian monk, wrote: "The truth can be a sword. If you use it with the desire to harm someone, it can actually become an evil. Never use truth this way. Always be motivated by a desire for good when you wield truth."[6]

Dr. Laura Schlessinger wisely says it this way: "Honesty means that everything you say must be true, not that everything that is true must be said."[7]

When we follow that advice, we'll also keep the intent of Ephesians 4:29, "Do not let any unwholesome talk come out of your mouths, but only what is helpful for building others up according to their needs, that it may benefit those who listen."

Gossip

If Gossip were a person, what do you suppose his biography would be like? Here's a possibility:

My name is Gossip. I have no respect for justice.
I maim without killing. I break hearts and ruin lives.
I am cunning and malicious and gather strength with age.
The more I am quoted, the more I am believed.
I flourish at every level of society.
My victims are helpless. They cannot protect themselves
    against me because I have no face.
To track me down is impossible. The harder you try, the
    more elusive I become.
I am nobody's friend.
Once I tarnish a reputation, it is never the same.
I topple governments, wreck marriages, and ruin careers—
    cause sleepless nights, heartaches, and indigestion.
I spawn suspicion and generate grief.
I make innocent people cry in their pillows.
Even my name hisses . . .
I make headlines and headaches.

—Anonymous

Alan Redpath gives us some similar fodder to chew on in his acronym "THINK."

        T Is it True?

        H Will it Help?

        I Is it Inspiring?

        N Is it Necessary?

        K Is it Kind?[8]

If we ask ourselves those questions before saying anything, we may find we have less to say! Proverbs 10:19 advises: "When words are many, sin is not absent, but he who holds his tongue is wise."

We should not pass along any information about a person

unless we have the person's permission to do so. We also should wait to share sensitive prayer requests about people until they've given us permission. If we suspect someone is trying to share a juicy bit of gossip, we should say something like, "Has so-and-so given you permission to share this with me? If not, I'd prefer hearing it from her or him directly."

I must admit, thinking of saying that makes me nervous. I don't consider myself an assertive person. I have a strong need to be accepted and therefore I wouldn't want to risk making someone peeved at me. But if I'm going to keep this Ninth Commandment, I must make the effort! And I must leave the results to God.

Several months ago, a woman approached me ready to give me the latest update on her friend who was being divorced by her husband. I knew it was because of this woman's own frustration that she wanted pass along the information, and so I had listened in the past. But having been recently reminded of the validity of the Ninth Commandment, I had determined not to be a part of it. She began to speak to me, but another friend came over and interrupted the conversation with a question. I quickly turned from the first woman and gave all my attention to the second person. The potential for gossip was defused. I thanked the Lord for His intervention as promised in 1 Corinthians 10:13. Maybe the next time I'll have to be more forceful, but I'm trusting He'll help then too.

You may also need to avoid or refuse to be friends with a person who lies or spreads gossip. If you are the source of the gossip or lies, then you can't separate from yourself, but you *can* break the habit! David A. Seamands gives the most powerful antidote to lying that I've ever heard and it's actually quite simple: apologize to the person you told the lie to![9]

This also makes me nervous! Having to take such a step could possibly cure me from lying altogether. The thought of admitting my wrong directly to the person I lied to is scary and humbling! I'm not into being humbled!

As we do our best to refrain from gossip, let's keep in mind a famous Hasidic story. A student has been spreading lies about his teacher. Eventually, the student realizes his error and goes to his teacher and confesses his sin, asking his teacher for forgiveness.

The teacher suggests, "If you want to make amends for what you've done, I recommend taking several feather pillows, cutting them open, and letting the wind disperse the feathers. Come and tell me when you've done that."

The student is relieved to think of such a simple consequence and does as he was told. He returns to the teacher who says, "Now, there's one more thing you need to do."

The student eagerly awaits his words.

"Go and gather up all those feathers."

The student is shocked. "But teacher, that's impossible. How can I do that? They have been scattered in every direction."

The teacher nods in agreement. "Now you're beginning to learn about the power of words. Once you have started or repeated a hurtful rumor and it spreads in all directions, it is very difficult to try to undo all the damage."

God tells us in the Ninth Commandment, "You shall not give false testimony against your neighbor." Let's stop casting those feathers to the wind and speak only the truth.

Inspecting the Damage

When we're whispering that tiny bit of gossip, we can't imagine the hurt it might cause. And when we're trying to defend ourselves by stretching the truth a bit, it just doesn't seem that harmful. Yet in God's eyes, a lie is a lie. Our words cannot be taken back. Once a lie is spoken, we give birth to a separate entity that we can no longer control.

Because of the potential harm that lying causes, God has heavy consequences for those who lie. Ananias and Sapphira in the early church were struck dead by God's judgement because they lied about the amount they'd given to the church from the sale of some property. Their sin wasn't in keeping back some of the money; they could choose to do whatever they wanted. Their sin was in claiming to have given it all to the common good of the church members when they hadn't. They paid for it with their lives.

Although I don't know of anyone who has died recently because of lying, there are other damaging consequences you or I might experience. Several years ago I attended a meeting of an organization that I had joined, and heard an announcement about the illness of one of the members. I whispered to the woman next to me, "What's that all about?"

She rolled her eyes and sneered, "She's getting meals brought in because of morning sickness." Evidently, she didn't consider that morning sickness warranted that kind of help.

When the list came by to sign up for providing a meal, I hesitated to sign up because of the woman's comment. Of course, I was still responsible for obeying God in what I chose to do, but if someone is easily influenced, she or he may not make a godly choice.

Church splits over doctrine or other (usually unimportant) issues cause people to fall away from the church. A church split can become an ugly example to unbelievers that "those Christians" just can't get along. Yet Jesus said that we should be known by our love. Instead, Satan uses lies to create division and strife.

All this damage and hurt is described in Scripture. Proverbs 25:18 tells us, "Like a club or a sword or a sharp arrow is the man who gives false testimony against his neighbor." Proverbs 16:28 gives us the results of gossip: "A perverse man stirs up dissension, and a gossip separates close friends."

When we're raked over the coals by unkind words or gossip, we can understand the meaning of Proverbs 30:14, "...those whose teeth are swords and whose jaws are set with knives to devour the poor from the earth, the needy from among mankind." And Proverbs 18:21 tells us the importance of our words.

"The tongue has the power of life and death, and those who love it will eat its fruit."

If we inspect the damage lies cause, we will begin to hold our tongue and taste the good fruit of self-control.

Search Yourself

Why do you think God hates dishonesty?
To what degree do you hate it?

⁓✶⁓

What helps you to hate dishonesty and what
prevents you from hating dishonesty?

⁓✶⁓

Someone has said, "If you tell the truth, you don't
ever have to remember the lie." How could the
truth of this adage motivate you to refrain from
telling a lie or from gossiping?

⁓✶⁓

If someone were to give you that trick question
about the man threatening to kill his wife (whom
you know is hiding in your closet), what would
you say to that angry man?

⁓✶⁓

Read Revelation 21:8. How could you use this
verse to help a person stop lying?

⁓✶⁓

What will you do to stop yourself fom lying and
spreading gossip?

Every increased possession

loads us with a

new weariness.

JOHN RUSKIN

RULE

X

Treasure the Gifts of God

YOU SHALL NOT COVET YOUR NEIGHBOR'S HOUSE.
YOU SHALL NOT COVET YOUR NEIGHBOR'S WIFE, OR
HIS MANSERVANT OR MAIDSERVANT,
HIS OX OR DONKEY,
OR ANYTHING THAT BELONGS TO YOUR NEIGHBOR.

EXODUS 20:17

When I was ten, I just knew that if Santa Claus gave me that new pink bike, I would be happy for the rest of my life. But when I received it, the happiness lasted no more than a few days.

When I was fifteen, I just knew that getting my driver's license would give me the joy I was looking for. When I received it, I did have fun driving, but still, it didn't do for me what I thought it would.

When I was twenty, I just knew that getting married to Larry would meet all my needs. Well, he was and is great, but Larry doesn't even try to meet all my needs!

When I was twenty-four, I just knew that becoming a mother would give me the ultimate happiness. Soon I had a baby and soon after that I realized how much work babies are. Far from being happy, sometimes I was frustrated!

By that time, I started getting a little wiser. Maybe all these things, expectations, and people weren't meant to be the source of my happiness. C. S. Lewis wrote, "What does not satisfy when we find it, was not the thing we were desiring."

As I turned my eyes from things and people to Jesus, I realized Jesus was the only faithful source of joy and fulfillment. Other things and people could give temporary joy, and sometimes God wanted them to do that, but He was the ultimate source.

Can you relate? Most people do. Though the longing for joy and contentment is always what motivates us, we go from object to object trying to find that joy, that place of peace and serenity. Though we may try several routes for getting it, we are always looking for contentment.

How's Your C.Q.?

What's your current contentment quotient (C.Q.)? Are you happy? Are you content? Are you satisfied? God had each of us in mind when He said, "Don't covet." Coveting is the opposite of contentment and satisfaction. Coveting says, "I'm not happy with what I've got so I want more, and I want it from you!" But God says in the tenth rule not to "set your desire" on those things you can't have.

The word for "covet" in Hebrew is *hamad* and it means "desire." Now this is not just a normal desire, because God created us with desires and those aren't wrong. God wants us to desire things like growth and goodness. *Hamad* refers to the kind of desire that wants what is not ours. When we want what is not ours, we break the tenth rule.

Carron says it this way: "I have found that if I am coveting something, then I am grumbling against God's perfect provision for me. If He hasn't given me something, then He knows that to have that thing is not in my best interests." Author John Sandford says, "We take by force of sin that which God would give us in time through grace."

David A. Seamands calls coveting "normal desire gone wrong."[1] One Bible commentator says the literal word-for-word translation is, "panting after something." Can't you just see that in yourself? I can. I've panted after being loved, getting new drapes, and having my yard professionally landscaped. I've panted after having that new dress in the department store window. Pant, pant, pant! If it begins to consume me, it's desire gone wrong!

Here are some verses worthy of contemplation and meditation:

Proverbs 21:26: All day long he craves for more, but the righteous give without sparing.

Micah 2:1–2: Woe to those who plan iniquity, to those who plot evil on their beds! At morning's light they carry it out because it is in their power to do it. They covet fields and seize them, and houses, and take them. They defraud a man of his home, a fellowman of his inheritance.

Colossians 3:5: Put to death, therefore, whatever belongs to your earthly nature: sexual immorality, impurity, lust, evil desires and greed, which is idolatry.

Placing Idols on the Shelf of Desire

The Rolling Stones sang, "I can't get no satisfaction." Even though they tried and they tried and they tried. They're right. Satisfaction doesn't come from those idols of desires gone wrong.

When I speak about contentment, I often ask my audience members, "Can you think of something on this earth that has given you long-term satisfaction?" They think long and hard and then there are usually a few things mentioned that fit the bill: usually photographs and momentos of significant events. That's valid. Most of us would lunge for the photo albums if our houses caught on fire. Those captured-on-film events and people are irreplaceable. But little else on earth gives us long-term satisfaction. Everything we buy can be replaced by something else. The majority of what we want today will soon be replaced by new things.

Listen to what some of my correspondents identified as "idols on the shelf of desire":

SUZANNE: "I used to enjoy the thrill of competitive sports, but it taught me to compare myself to the sportsman across from me. In other areas of life, I found comparisons becoming my idol. 'Her husband is more caring.' 'My co-worker is more successful.' 'Their child is more obedient.' Only when I realized God didn't want me to compare did I take those idols off the shelf. His plan is designed uniquely for me."

IRENE: "Coveting is always selfish. One time in my married life I wanted more attention from my husband. The more I craved, the less I got. I realized I couldn't make him do something on demand. The attention came when I became satisfied in our relationship as it existed. "

Billy Graham says, "Many people ask about Christianity the same thing they ask about everything else today: 'What's in it for me?' In our selfishness, we think of God as we think of everyone else. What can He contribute to us, personally? In other words, we want God to be our servant."[2]

Several years before her death, author Sally Conway wrote:

> Shortly after Jim and I were married, I started picking on
> Jim's grammar. I had been an English major, and he had
> to be tutored in English to make it through graduate
> school. Consequently, I had a terrible disrespect for him
> and nit-picked his every lapse in writing or speaking. Fi-
> nally, God got the message through to me: "Why don't
> you appreciate Jim's spiritual maturity, his sensitivity to
> people's needs, his sense of humor and creative ideas?
> Why not admire his good qualities instead of picking at
> his weak grammar skills?" I took it to heart, and sud-
> denly found I was married to a wonderful man with many
> great talents!

For Sally, her idol was correcting her husband's grammar.

In each of these people, there was an underlying belief about
God that encouraged their covetousness. You and I can believe wrong ideas about God too. Let's examine our concep-
tions of God.

Either Except or Accept

One misconception about God that can give rise to coveting
is the belief that God is stingy or the idea that He doesn't
really want what's best for us. We might fall into the temptation of thinking God wants to poke at us a bit for the sake of
poking at us. We think things like, "If God really loved me,
He wouldn't keep that from me." Coveting always focuses
on the *except*. "God, you've given me everything *except* that!"

In contrast to coveting's *except*, contentment says *accept*.
"Whatever you desire for me, Lord, I'll *accept* it." Contentment, the goal of the tenth rule, says that God knows what's
best for me and I can trust Him. He sees the big picture while
my vision is small and scratched. If God withholds some-

thing, then it must be because He knows very well it's not the best thing for me.

Years ago, when I prayed for instantaneous deliverance from my anger, I couldn't comprehend why God wouldn't answer in the affirmative. After all, He didn't want me to be angry; my frustration didn't bring Him glory. My patience would. But as I began to see how that God wanted to bring me through a process of growth, I rejoiced because I was learning things that could be passed along to others.

What do you desire that seems logical, even spiritually beneficial, but that God isn't giving you? In what way is Satan hissing that God wants to keep something good from you? Can you trust that God knows best? He does.

Contentment and Godliness

God wants us to be joyful and fulfilled, that's why He gave us His ten rules. He knows that envy, the kissing cousin of coveting, rots the bones (Proverbs 14:30). Coveting steals our joy and makes us unhappy. Things don't satisfy us like we think they will.

Connie discovered that. She wrote me, "The older I become, the more I realize the unimportance of things. Having to go through my parents' and aunts' things after their deaths made me realize that the truly important things are the treasures that are sent on ahead to heaven. I once coveted my friend's beautiful home until I saw the way her husband mistreated her. Now I wouldn't trade places with her for anything! The finest house is not worth my loving, caring husband."

It's all a matter of perspective, isn't it? The more we have, the more care it takes, the more money it requires. And if we covet our best friend's spouse and get him, then we adopt the pain of divorce and damaged relationships.

It's interesting that coveting and adultery go together. In fact, the tenth rule forbids the attitude that can lead us to break the other commandments. Coveting, for example, is an attitude that can give rise to adultery, stealing, lying, and murder. It can even cause us to dishonor our father and mother if they can't give us what we crave. And if we're not content, we've got to work on Sunday to earn more money to buy more. And if we think God isn't truly God, we set up idols and bad mouth Him to others for being insensitive to our needs. We've ended up breaking all the commandments because we wanted what we wanted!

No wonder Paul wrote, "But godliness with contentment is great gain" (1 Timothy 6:6). They go together! When we're content and fighting those covetous passions, we will enjoy a greater godliness. That's the promise of the Ten Commandments and God's desire for us.

Cultivate the Soil of Contentment

We can enjoy greater godliness through choosing contentment. Yes, like so many things, contentment is a choice. You and I can choose to be joyful and happy regardless of our circumstances or how other people are treating us. I'm not talking about an outward happiness that comes and goes depending on the outcome of our day. It's a happiness that knows God is in charge. How can we keep that perspective?

First, by making it a goal. Jeanie says, "I have struggled with contentment. It is a real obstacle to practicing the presence of the Lord, glorifying Him and loving Him with my whole heart. I have written a goal in my journal to 'cultivate the habit of seeking nothing but God in all that I do.' He seems to respond and tells me to choose less and not more and then He will bless me with more. Ironic isn't it? The more I focus on being contented in Him, the less the world seems desirable yet my blessings increase."

As we make contentment a goal, we can remember that it is indeed a process, something learned. I take great comfort in the fact that even the Apostle Paul said in Philippians 4:11 that he is *learning* contentment. "I am not saying this because I am in need, for I have learned to be content whatever the circumstances. I know what it is to be in need, and I know what it is to have plenty. I have learned the secret of being content in any and every situation, whether well fed or hungry, whether living in plenty or in want. I can do everything through him who gives me strength" (Philippians 4:11–13).

Paul experienced every degree of need and plenty and found he could choose by God's strength to be content. You and I can do the same by focusing on the positive instead of the negative. Are your husband's long hours driving you crazy? Choose to see how you can minister to others with the time you have to yourself. Focus on the little things that bring joy rather than waiting for that big event that never comes.

Another idea is to follow Alicia's goal of setting priorities. She says, "Another account manager in our office seems to work half as much as I do, and is making at least twenty-five percent more. I watch how he works when he's in the office and get so frustrated that he's making sales and I'm not. It seems so easy to become envious of others. When I become discontent, I have to take a step back and remember what is important. I am not here to outdo my co-workers. I am not alive to make more money. I am not here to keep up with the Joneses. I am here to love the Lord my God with all my heart, and love my neighbor as myself. When I remember why I'm here, my envy disappears, and contentment radiates in my life again."

Alicia is wise in seeing what's really important. We can ask ourselves, "Will this be important five years from now? Will this be important in heaven?" If what we're seeking will evaporate or disappear in a short time, then it certainly can't supply the satisfaction we desire.

Dianne shared with me another key for choosing contentment. She prays a blessing upon any whom she starts to envy despite her mother's bad influence. Dianne and her family were very poor and her mother frequently complained or gossiped about the wealthy people in their town. If someone drove by in a big car, her mother would find something wrong with it. If another woman bought groceries that Dianne's mother couldn't afford, Dianne's mother would whisper to her children something bad she'd heard about that woman.

Dianne says, "I have overcome my mother's prejudice, realizing it is unfair to lump all people into one category. Over the years, I've met nice wealthy people, mean poor people, and vice versa. I decided wealth or poverty do not determine a person's worth. If I find myself resenting or coveting what others have, I pray God will continue to bless them. I have many wealthy friends now and believe I have overcome the wrong attitudes my mother had."

Making that choice to bless and not curse sets us free from coveting. It reminds us that God chooses the circumstances for each of us and desires only our good. Of course, that doesn't mean we shouldn't use our money wisely or that we should make unwise investment choices.

God tells us to obey this tenth rule and that means making a choice. Maybe hearing Charles Swindoll's perspective will help us:

> Someday when the kids are grown, things are going to be a lot different. The garage won't be full of bikes, electric train tracks on plywood, sawhorses surrounded by chunks of two-by-fours, unfinished "experimental projects," and the rabbit cage.
>
> Someday when the kids are grown, the kitchen will be incredibly neat. The sink will stay free of sticky dishes, the garbage disposal won't get choked on rubber bands or paper cups, and we won't lose the tops to jelly jars, catsup bottles, the peanut butter, the margarine, or the mustard.

Someday when the kids are grown, the instrument called a "telephone" will actually be available. It won't look like it's growing from a teenager's ear.

Someday when the kids are grown, I'll be able to see through the car windows. Fingerprints, tongue licks, sneaker footprints, and dog tracks (nobody knows how) will be conspicuous by their absence.

Someday when the kids are grown, we will return to normal conversations. You know, just plain American talk. "Gross" won't punctuate every sentence seven times.

Yes, someday when the kids are grown, things are going to be a lot different. The house will be quiet . . . and calm . . . and always clean . . . and empty . . . and filled with memories . . . and lonely . . . and we won't like that at all. And we'll spend our time not looking forward to *Someday* but looking back to *Yesterday*. And thinking, "Maybe we can baby-sit the grandkids and get some life back in this place for a change !"[3]

Let's choose to avoid the attitudes of "someday" and "except" and instead, choose life through contentment.

Search Yourself

How do you define coveting and to what degree do you find it in your life?

✦

What is contentment to you? How is your "C.Q.," your contentment quotient?

✦

If you fall into times of coveting, what is the object of your desires most often?

✦

What circumstances seem to diminish your ability to choose contentment?

✦

What is your attitude about God's generosity and how does that influence your "C.Q."?

✦

What one thing will you do or think in order to increase your "C.Q."?

Love, and do
what thou wilt.

ST. AUGUSTINE

Afterword

It's been quite a ride through God's ten rules. I didn't expect to learn as much as I did. How about you? I feel like our Lord has covered every important aspect of life. He is so thorough and gentle. He doesn't hit us over the head but firmly says, "Precious one, I know what's best for you. Now go to it!"

As I mentioned in the beginning, the rules we've studied are the basis for loving God and then loving others. In many ways they are the foundation of Jesus' teaching. The Ten Commandments give us the basis for setting our priorities and balancing our lives. Some time ago, I drove down a newly paved road on which the yellow lines hadn't yet been painted. It was a multi-laned highway and I felt nervous. As I drove along, I wondered whether I was in the correct lane. I stared at the driver next to me and wanted to shout, "Now stay over there because this is my lane." But what lane? There weren't any lines. No one really knew if they were doing the right thing or not.

In the same way, if God hadn't given us the Ten Rules, we wouldn't know whether we were doing the right thing or not. I imagine we would want to tell everyone else how they should drive down the road of life, but all the time we would be without a firm foundation for doing so.

We can thank God for these rules. Because of them, we know when we've gone astray and how to get back in the right lane. We know how to love God and love others.

As you consider the challenges we've faced in these rules, allow God to let them permeate your being and thinking slowly. Like a dripping faucet (without the irritation), let the Lord seep His truths deep into your soul. It may take time but that's okay. Don't expect perfect compliance immediately. Over and over again meditate on these Ten Rules for joy and fulfillment. Only then will they have a lasting impact upon your life and the lives of those around you.

And as Paul said in his second letter to the Corinthians, "May the grace of the Lord Jesus Christ, and the love of God, and the fellowship of the Holy Spirit be with you all." Amen.

Endnotes

INTRODUCTION

1. "Most Say Ten Commandments Apply to Self, Not Others" (PRRC Emerging Trends, published by the Princeton Religion Research center, Vol. 10, No. 4, April 1988).
2. Michael Cromartie, "How We Muddle Our Morals," *Christianity Today*, May/June 1996, Vol. 2, No. 3), 14.
3. Charles R. Swindoll, General Editor, *The Living Insights Study Bible* (Grand Rapids, Mich.: Zondervan, 1996), 82.
4. William Law, *Mystical Writings*, quoted in Bernard Bangley, *Near to the Heart of God, Compiled and Prepared for Modern Readers* (Wheaton, Il.: Harold Shaw Publishers, 1998), January 19. Used by permission.
5. Richard C. Halverson, *Perspective* (a letter of Concern Ministries, May 6, 1992).
6. Bernard of Clairvaux, *On Loving God*, quoted in Bernard Bangley, *Near to the Heart of God*, January 6. Used by permission.
7. Gwen Shamblin, *Weigh Down* (New York,: Doubleday, 1997), 189.
8. John R.W. Stott, *The Message of Galatians: Only One Way* (Downers Grove, Il.: Inter-Varsity Press, 1968), 93.
9. Joy Davidman, *Smoke on the Mountain* (Philadelphia, Pa.: The Westminster Press, 1953), 16. Used by permission.
10. Charles R. Swindoll, *God's Masterwork Bible Study Guide, Volume One* (Anaheim, Ca.: Insight for Living, 1996), 24.
11. Francis A. Schaeffer, *The Mark of the Christian* (Downers Grove, Il.: InterVarsity Press, and L'Abri Fellowship, 1970), adapted from article "The Mark of the Christian," *Christianity Today Magazine*, 1995.
12. Ronald B. Allen, "In His Law, the Surprise of His Grace" (*Moody*, December, 1989), 42.

CHAPTER 1

1. John H. Timmerman, *Do We Still Need the Ten Commandments?* (Minneapolis, Minn.: Augsburg, 1997), 24. Used by permission.
2. Joy Davidman, *Smoke on the Mountain* (Philadelphia, Pa.: The Westminster Press, 1953), 22. Used by permission.
3. Timmerman, *Do We Still Need the Ten Commandments?*, 25. Used by permission.
4. Alan Redpath, *Law and Liberty* (Old Tappan, N.J.: Revell, 1978), 16.
5. Larry Crabb, *Effective Biblical Counseling* (Grand Rapids, Mich.: Zondervan, 1977), 61.
6. Gregg Lewis, "Tom and Alicia Landry" (*Marriage Partnership*, Winter, 1991), 47-48.
7. Redpath, *Law and Liberty*, 17.
8. Martin Luther, *Instruction in Christian Love*, quoted in Bernard Bangley, *Near to the Heart of God*, January 28. Used by permission.
9. Dr. Laura Schlessinger and Rabbi Stewart Vogel, *The Ten Commandments: The Significance of God's Laws in Everyday Life* (New York: Cliff Street Books, 1998), 11-12.
10. Chuck Swindoll, *Living Above the Level of Mediocrity* (Dallas, Tex.: Word, 1987) 114.
11. J. I. Packer, *Growing In Christ* (Wheaton, Il.: Crossway Books, 1994), 229. Used by permission.

CHAPTER 2

1. Packer, *Growing In Christ*, 244. Used by permission.
2. R. Kent Hughes, *Disciplines of Grace* (Wheaton, Il,: Crossway Books, 1993), 45
3. Timmerman, *Do We Still Need the Ten Commandments?*, 40. Used by permission.
4. Davidman, *Smoke on the Mountain*, 33. Used by permission.
5. Stuart Briscoe, *Playing by the Rules* (Old Tappan, N.J.: Revell, 1986), 38. Used by permission.
6. Redpath, *Law and Liberty*, 27.
7. David A. Seamands, *God's Blueprint for Living* (Wilmore, Ken.: Bristol Books, 1988), 42. Used by permission.
8. Briscoe, *Playing by the Rules*, 43. Used by permission.
9. J. I. Packer, *Knowing God* (Downers Grove, Il.: Inter-Varsity Press, 1973), 42.

10. William Law, *Mystical Writings*, quoted in Bernard Bangley, *Near to the Heart of God*, January 19. Used by permission.
11. Packer, *Growing In Christ*, 243-244. Used by permission.
12. Seamands, *God's Blueprint for Living*, 27-28. Used by permission.
13. C. H. Spurgeon, quoted in J. I. Packer, *Knowing God*, 13.
14. A. W. Tozer, *The Knowledge of the Holy* (New York: Harper & Row, 1961), 16.
15. Briscoe, *Playing by the Rules*, 45. Used by permission.
16. Copyright, 1994, Roger Barrier.
17. Copyright, 1998, Stacey Padrick. Used by permission.

CHAPTER 3

1. Seamands, *God's Blueprint for Living*, 53. Used by permission.
2. Liz Curtis Higgs, *Mirror, Mirror on the Wall, Have I Got News For You!* (Nashville, Tenn.: Thomas Nelson, 1997), 24.
3. Briscoe, *Playing by the Rules*, 54. Used by permission.
4. Timmerman, *Do We Still Need the Ten Commandments?*, 53. Used by permission.
5. Billy Graham, *Till Armageddon* (Waco, Tex.: Word, 1981), 61.
6. Josh Getlin, "God, Money: New Twist on an Old Theme," *Los Angeles Times*, June 22, 1999, A1.
7. Timmerman, *Do We Still Need the Ten Commandments?*, 53. Used by permission.
8. Kay Arthur, *Lord, I Want to Know You* (Sisters, Ore.: Multnomah, 1992), 50.
9. Brother Lawrence, *The Practice of the Presence of God*, quoted in Bernard Bangley, *Near to the Heart of God* (Harold Shaw Publishers), April 6. Used by permission.

CHAPTER 4

1. Max Lucado, *He Still Moves Stones* (Dallas, Tex.: Word, 1993), 128.
2. Schlessinger and Vogel, *The Ten Commandments: The Significance of God's Laws in Everyday Life*, 107.
3. Seamands, *God's Blueprint for Living*, 67. Used by permission.
4. Packer, *Growing In Christ*, 253. Used by permission.
5. Arthur, *Lord, I Want to Know You*, 122-123.
6. Seamands, *God's Blueprint for Living*, 68-69. Used by permission.
7. Patsy Clairmont, *Normal is Just a Setting on Your Dryer*

(Colorado Springs, Colo.: Focus on the Family Publishing, 1993), 13.

8. Redpath, *Law and Liberty*, 50.
9. Robin Jones Gunn, *Mothering by Heart* (Sisters, Ore.: Multnomah, 1996), 17. Used by permission.
10. Edith Schaeffer, *Lifelines* (Westchester, Il.: Crossway Books, 1982), 98.

CHAPTER 5

1. Davidman, *Smoke on the Mountain*, 83. Used by permission.
2. Seamands, *God's Blueprint for Living*, 83. Used by permission.
3. Schlessinger and Vogel, *The Ten Commandments: The Significance of God's Laws in Everyday Life*, 169.
4. Barbara Johnson, *Mama, Get the Hammer! There's A Fly on Papa's Head!* (Dallas, Tex.: Word, 1994), 91.
5. Copyright, 1998, Dee Hyatt, featured in *God's Abundance for Women* (Lancaster, Pa.: Starburst Publishers). Used by permission.
6. Lucado, *He Still Moves Stones*, 44.
7. Briscoe, *Playing by the Rules*, 92. Used by permission.
8. Lucado, *He Still Moves Stones*, 44.
9. Copyright, 1991, Jerry Cecil. Used by permission.
10. Edwin Hubbell Chapin, quoted in Leonard Felder, Ph.D, *The Ten Challenges* (New York: Harmony Books, 1997), 109.
11. David A. Seamands, *Healing for Damaged Emotions* (Wheaton, Il.: Victor, 1981), 139. Used by permission.

CHAPTER 6

1. Schlessinger and Vogel, *The Ten Commandments: The Significance of God's Laws in Everyday Life*, 130.
2. Davidman, *Smoke on the Mountain*, 75. Used by permission.
3. Briscoe, *Playing by the Rules*, 98. Used by permission.
4. Found on the Internet.
5. Frederica Mathewes-Green, "Why Women Choose Abortion" (*Christianity Today Magazine*, September, 1995). Found on the Internet.
6. Gary L. Thomas, "Deadly Compassion," *Christianity Today*, June 16, 1997, Vol. 41, No. 7, 14.
7. Copyright 1996, June Cerza Kolf, from *God's Vitamin "C" for the Spirit* (Lancaster, Pa.: Starburst Publishers). Used by permission.

8. Thomas à Kempis, *The Imitation of Christ*, quoted in Bernard Bangley, *Near to the Heart of God*, April 14. Used by permission.
9. Billy Graham, *Unto the Hills* (Dallas, Tex.: Word, 1986), Page number unknown.
10. Martin Luther, *Table Talk*, quoted in *Near to the Heart of God, Compiled and Prepared for Modern Readers*, January 14. Used by permission.
11. Redpath, *Law and Liberty*, 77.
12. Lawrence Scupoli, *The Spiritual Combat*, quoted in *Near to the Heart of God, Compiled and Prepared for Modern Readers*, March 20. Used by permission.

CHAPTER 7

1. Bill Hybels and Rob Wilkins, *Tender Love* (Chicago, Il.: Moody, 1993), 75.
2. Seamands, *God's Blueprint for Living*, 103. Used by permission.
3. Liz Curtis Higgs, *Mirror, Mirror on the Wall, Have I Got News for You!*, 54.
4. Hybels and Wilkins, *Tender Love*, 32.
5. C. S. Lewis, *Mere Christianity* (New York, NY: Touchstone, Simon & Schuster, 1996), 92.
6. Gary Richmond, *The Divorce Decision* (Waco, Tex.: Word, 1988), 21.
7. Ibid., 40.
8. Jim Burns, "Let's Talk," *Campus Life Magazine* (November, 1995) 8.
9. Lucado, *He Still Moves Stones* (Dallas, Tex,: Word, 1993), 28.
10. Hughes, *Disciplines of Grace*, 132.
11. Ann Landers, *Los Angeles Times*, October 27, 1999.
12. Schaeffer, *Lifelines*, 156.
13. Robertson McQuilkin, adapted from "Muriel's Blessing," *Christianity Today*, February 5, 1996.

CHAPTER 8

1. Doug Sherman and William Hendricks, *Keeping Your Ethical Edge Sharp* (Colorado Springs, Colo.: Nav Press, 1990), 71-72.
2. Redpath, *Law and Liberty*, 92.
3. Martin Luter, *Small Catechism*, quoted in John H. Timmerman, *Do We Still Need the Ten Commandments?*, 134.

4. Graham, *Till Armageddon*, 63.
5. Patsy Clairmont, *Normal is Just a Setting on Your Dryer*, (Colorado Springs, Colo.: Focus on the Family Publishing, 1993), 30.
6. Seamands, *God's Blueprint for Living*, 116-117. Used by permission.
7. Schaeffer, *Lifelines*, 170.
8. Chuck Colson, "BreakPoint with Chuck Colson," Prison Fellowship Ministries. Found on internet.

CHAPTER 9

1. Leonard Felder, Ph.D., *The Ten Challenges*, 183.
2. Seamands, *God's Blueprint for Living*, 122. Used by permission.
3. Patsy Clairmont, *It's About Home* (Ann Arbor, Mich.: Vine/Servant, 1998), 121.
4. Thomas a' Kempis, *The Imitation of Christ*, quoted in Bangley, *Near to the Heart of God*, February 18. Used by permission.
5. Packer, *Growing In Christ*, 273. Used by permission.
6. Guigo I, *Meditations*, quoted in *Near to the Heart of God*, April 4. Used by permission.
7. Schlessinger and Vogel, *The Ten Commandments: The Significance of God's Laws in Everyday Life*, 287.
8. Redpath, *Law and Liberty*, 107-108.
9. Seamands, *God's Blueprint for Living*, 124. Used by permission.

CHAPTER 10

1. Seamands, *God's Blueprint for Living*, 134. Used by permission.
2. Graham, *Till Armageddon*, 64.
3. Chuck Swindoll, *Standing Out* (Portland, Oreg.: Multnomah Press, 1979), 100-102.

Other Books by Starburst Publishers®

(partial listing – full list available upon request)

Since Life Isn't A Game, These Are God's Rules—*Kathy Collard Miller*
Subtitled: Finding Joy & Fulfillment0 in God's Ten Commandments. We often hear life being referred to as a *game*, but we know this is not really true. In life there is only one set of rules and those are God's. God gave us the Ten Commandments for our good—to protect and guide us. In this book, Kathy Collard Miller explains the meaning of each of the Ten Commandments and illustrates how they are relevant in today's life. Each chapter includes Scripture and quotes from some of our most beloved Christian authors including Billy Graham, Patsy Clairmont, Liz Curtis Higgs, and more! Sure to renew your understanding of God's rules.
(cloth)   ISBN 189201615X   **$16.95**

God's Abundance for Women—*Compiled by Kathy Collard Miller*
Subtitled: Devotions for a More Meaningful Life. Following the success of *God's Abundance*, this book will touch women of all ages as they seek a more meaningful life. Essays from our most beloved Christian authors exemplify how to gain the abundant life that Jesus promised through trusting Him to fulfill our every need. Each story is enhanced with Scripture, quotes, and practical tips providing brief, yet deeply spiritual reading.
(cloth)   ISBN 1892016141   **$19.95**

More God's Abundance—*Compiled by Kathy Collard Miller*
Subtitled: Joyful Devotions for Every Season. Editor Kathy Collard Miller responds to the tremendous success of *God's Abundance* with a fresh collection of stories based on God's Word for a simpler life. Includes stories from our most beloved Christian writers such as: Liz Curtis Higgs and Patsy Clairmont that are combined ideas, tips, quotes, and scripture.
(cloth)   ISBN 1892016133   **$19.95**

God's Abundance—*Edited by Kathy Collard Miller*
Over 100,000 sold! This day-by-day inspirational is a collection of thoughts by leading Christian writers such as Patsy Clairmont, Jill Briscoe, Liz Curtis Higgs, and Naomi Rhode. *God's Abundance* is based on God's Word for a simpler, yet more abundant life. Learn to make all aspects of your life—personal, business, financial, relationships, even housework a "spiritual abundance of simplicity."
(cloth)   ISBN 0914984977   **$19.95**

Promises of God's Abundance—*Edited by Kathy Collard Miller*
Subtitled: *For a More Meaningful Life.* The Bible is filled with God's promises for an abundant life. *Promises of God's Abundance* is written in the same way as the best-selling *God's Abundance*. It will help you discover these promises and show you how simple obedience is the key to an abundant life. Scripture, questions for growth, and a simple thought for the day will guide you to a more meaningful life.
(trade paper)   ISBN 0914984-098   **$9.95**

Stories of God's Abundance—*Compiled by Kathy Collard Miller*

Subtitled: for a More Joyful Life . Following the success of *God's Abundance* (100,000 sold), this book is filled with beautiful, inspirational, real life stories of God, Scriptures, and insights that any reader can apply to their daily lives. Renew your faith in life's small miracles and challenge yourself to allow God to lead the way as you find the source of abundant living for all your relationships. (trade paper) ISBN 1892016060 **$12.95**

God's Unexpected Blessings—*Edited by Kathy Collard Miller*

Over 50,000 sold! Learn to see the unexpected blessings in life. These individual essays describe experiences that seem negative on the surface but are something God has used for good in our lives or to benefit others. Witness God at work in our lives. Learn to trust God in action. Realize that we always have a choice to learn and benefit from these experiences by letting God prove His promise of turning all things for our good. (cloth) ISBN 0914984071 **$18.95**

Why Fret That God Stuff?—*Edited by Kathy Collard Miller*

Subtitled: *Stories of Encouragement to Help You Let Go and Let God Take Control of All Things in Your Life.* Occasionally, we all become overwhelmed by the everyday challenges of our lives: hectic schedules, our loved ones' needs, unexpected expenses, a sagging devotional life. *Why Fret That God Stuff* is the perfect beginning to finding joy and peace for the real world! (trade paper) ISBN 0914984-500 **$12.95**

Seasons of a Woman's Heart—*Compiled by Lynn D. Morrissey*

Subtitled: A Daybook of Stories and Inspiration. A woman's heart is complex. This daybook of stories, quotes, scriptures, and daily reflections will inspire and refresh. Christian women share their heart-felt thoughts on Seasons of Faith, Growth, Guidance, Nurturing, and Victory. Including Christian women's writers such as Kay Arthur, Emilie Barnes, Luci Swindoll, Jill Briscoe, Florence Littauer, and Gigi Graham Tchividjian. (cloth) ISBN 1892016036 **$18.95**

The *God's Word for the Biblically-Inept*™ series is already a best-seller with over 100,000 books sold! Designed to make reading the Bible easy, educational and fun! This series of verse-by-verse Bible studies, Topical Studies and Overviews mixes scholarly information from experts with helpful icons, illustrations, sidebars and time lines. It's the Bible made easy!

The Bible—God's Word for the Biblically-Inept™—*Larry Richards*

An excellent book to start leaning the entire Bible. Get the basics or the indepth information you are seeking with this user-friendly overview. From Creation to Christ to the Millenium, learning the Bible has never been easier. (trade paper) ISBN 0914984551 **$16.95**

Revelation—God's Word for the Biblically-Inept™—*Daymond R. Duck*

End-time Bible Prophecy, expert Daymond Duck leads us verse-by-verse through one of the Bible's most confusing books. Follow the experts as they forge their way through the captivating prophecies of Revelation! (trade paper) ISBN 0914984985 **$16.95**

Daniel—God's Word for the Biblically-Inept™—*Daymond R. Duck*
Daniel is a book of prophecy and the key to understanding the mysteries of the Tribulation and End-Time events. This verse-by-verse commentary combines humor and scholasticism to get at the essentials of scripture. Perfect for those who want to know the truth about the Antichrist.
(trade paper)   ISBN 0914984489   **$16.95**

Health and Nutrition—God's Word for the Biblically-Inept™
—*Kathleen O'Bannon Baldinger*
The Bible is full of God's rules for good health! Kathleen Baldinger reveals scientific evidence that proves the diet and health principles outlined in the Bible are the best for total health. Learn about the Bible Diet, the food pyramid and fruits and vegetable from the Bible! Experts include: Pamela Smith, Julian Whitaker, Kenneth Cooper, and TD Jakes.
(trade paper)   ISBN 0914984055   **$16.95**

Men of the Bible—God's Word for the Biblically-Inept™
—*D. Larry Miller*
Benefit from the life experiences of the powerful men of the Bible! Learn how the inspirational struggles of men such as Moses, Daniel, Paul, and David parallel the struggles of today's man. It will inspire and build Christian character for any reader.
(trade paper)   ISBN 1892016079   **$16.95**

Women of the Bible—God's Word for the Biblically-Inept™
—*Kathy Collard Miller*
Finally, a Bible perspective just for women! Gain valuable insight from the successes and struggles of such women as Eve, Esther, Mary, Sarah, and Rebekah. Interesting icons like: Get Close to God, Build Your Spirit and Grow your Marriage will make incorporating God's Word into your daily life easy.   (trade paper)   ISBN 0914984063   **$16.95**

What's in the Bible for™ Women—*Georgia Curtis Ling*
What does the Bible have to say to women? Find out in the second release from the **What's in the Bible for...™** series. Women of all ages will find Biblical insight on the topics that are meaningful to them in six simple sections including: Faith, Family, Friends, Fellowship, Freedom, and Femininity. From the editors of the *God's Word for the Biblically-Inept™* series, this book also uses illustrations, bullet points, chapter summaries, and icons to make understanding God's Word easier than ever!
(trade paper)   ISBN 1-892016-11-7   **$16.95**

The Weekly Feeder—*Cori Kirkpatrick*
Subtitled: A Revolutionary Shopping, Cooking and Meal Planning System.
The Weekly Feeder is a revolutionary meal planning system that will make preparing home-cooked dinners more convenient than ever. At the beginning of each week, simply choose one of the eight pre-planned weekly menus, tear-out the corresponding grocery list, do your shopping and whip up a great meal in less than 45 minutes! The author's household management tips, equipment checklists, and nutrition information make this system a must have for any busy family. Also included with every recipe is a personal anecdote from the author emphasizing the importance of good food, a healthy family and a well-balanced life.
(trade paper)   ISBN 1892016095   **$16.95**

God Stories—*Donna I. Douglas*

Subtitled: They're So Amazing, Only God Could Make Them Happen. Famous individuals share their personal, true-life experiences with God in this beautiful new book! Find out how God has touched the life of top recording artists, professional athletes and other newsmakers such as: Jessi Colter, Deana Carter, Ben Vereen, Stephanie Zimbalist, Cindy Morgan, Sheila E., Joe Jacoby, Cheryl Landon, Brett Butler, Clifton Taulbert, Babbie Mason, Michael Medved, Sandi Patty, Charlie Daniels and more! Their stories are intimate, poignant, and sure to inspire and motivate you as you listen for God's message in your own life! (cloth) ISBN 1892016117 **$18.95**

More of Him, Less of Me—*Jan Christensen*

Subtitled: *A Daybook of My Personal Insights, Inspirations & Meditations on the Weigh Down™ Diet.* The insight shared in this year-long daybook of inspiration will encourage you on your weight-loss journey, bring you to a deeper relationship with God, and help you improve any facet of your life. Each page includes an essay, Scripture and a tip-of-the-day that will encourage and uplift you as you trust God to help you achieve your proper weight. Perfect for companion guide for anyone on the Weigh Down™ diet! (cloth) ISBN 1892016001 **$17.95**

Desert Morsels—*Jan Christiansen*

A Journal with Encouraging Tidbits from My Journey on the Weigh Down™ Diet. When Jan Christiansen set out to lose weight on the Weigh Down™ Diet she got more than she bargained for! In addition to *losing* over 35 pounds and *gaining* a closer relationship with God, Jan discovered a gift—her ability to entertain and comfort fellow dieters! Jan's inspiring website led to the release of her best-selling first book, *More of Him, Less of Me.* Now, Jan serves another helping of *her* wit and *His* wisdom in this lovely companion journal. Includes inspiring Scripture, insightful comments, stories from readers, room for the reader's personal reflection and **P**lenty of **Attitude** (p-attitude). (cloth) ISBN 1892016214 **$16.95**

Purchasing Information:
www.starburstpublishers.com

Books are available from your favorite bookstore, either from current stock or special order. To assist bookstore in locating your selection be sure to give title, author, and ISBN #. If unable to purchase from the bookstore you may order direct from STARBURST PUBLISHERS. When ordering enclose full payment plus shipping and handling as follows: Post Office (4th Class)—$3.00 (Up to $20.00), $4.00 ($20.01-$50.00), 8% ($50.01 and Up); UPS—$4.50 (Up to $20.00), $6.00 ($20.01-$50.00), 12% ($50.01 and Up); Canada—$5.00 (Up to $35.00), 15% ($35.01 and Up); Overseas (Surface)—$5.00 (Up to $25.00), 20% ($25.01 and Up). Payment in U.S. Funds only. Please allow two to three weeks minimum (longer overseas) for delivery. Make checks payable to and mail to: STARBURST PUBLISHERS, P.O. Box 4123, LANCASTER, PA 17604. Credit card orders may also be placed by calling 1-800-441-1456 (credit card orders only), Mon-Fri, 8:30 a.m. to 5:30 p.m. Eastern Standard Time. Prices subject to change without notice. Catalog available for a 9 x 12 self-addressed envelope with 4 first-class stamps.